EMPOWER
YOUR CHILDREN

Teach Kids to Ask Meaningful

Questions, Recognize Bias, and

Stand Up for Themselves

Thomas Rowley PhD

EMPOWER YOUR CHILDREN
Teach Kids to Ask Meaningful Questions, Recognize Bias, and Stand up for Themselves

ISBN: 978-1-7370353-4-3 Teacher's Guide

978-1-7370353-2-9 e-book

978-1-7370353-3-6 paperback edition

978-1-7370353-5-0 hardback edition

LUUN 2021919119

Dedication

This book is dedicated to the thousand plus students I've had the privilege to share what I know with you over the past four decades or so. To see those 'aha moments' when the light of understanding comes on, and the evidence at the conclusion of a course that your repertoire of skills has grown, and you have the ability to properly apply them is what kept me returning to the classroom. Thank you.

My thanks in advance to all the parents, grandparents, teachers and counselors, friends and colleagues who read this book and share what they learn about being a responsible adult and practice the techniques of a respectful skeptic in your discussions with others. It will make a difference in your life and the lives of those with whom you interact. My aspiration is for our youth to be well-informed with facts. If we practice asking the questions the book recommends, each of us will have a positive impact on the world in which our children and their cohorts become thoughtful, engaged, and aware adults.

My gratitude goes out to the coaches and fellow authors at the Self- Publishing School whose insights and inputs made this a much better focused book.

Free Gift

*T*hank you for purchasing Empower Your Children. As a gift for purchase, I'm offering a free worksheet on *How To Become A Respectful Skeptic.* To get your copy go to

https://www.subscribepage.com/eyc

HOW TO BECOME A RESPECTFUL SKEPTIC

Ask yourself if you are asking following Four W questions on a consistent basis to be confident that you are making choices based on valid information from trusted sources

Says Who?

☐ Determine the real source and reliability of the information you hear on the news, read, or see on the internet?

Why Should I Care?

☐ Determine if the information while interesting has a direct impact on you or the lives of those you care about? If not, move on

Why Should I Believe You?

☐ Determine if the source of the information has any special expertise or experience that could give them any valuable insight?

Where's The Proof?

☐ Verify the credibility of the original source information by asking if there is objective evidence or more importantly, if there are conflicting conclusions based on the same idea.

Ask those Four W questions.
Your life will be better for It

PREFACE TO REVISED EDITION

The edition you have in your hands is titled more precisely–
Empower Your Children.

What I saw and heard from other educational professionals
encouraged me to look past the clearly identifiable problems
that had festered since the 1960s and to put into practice my
experience as a problem solver. That led to the publication of
this book with its original title *Blame It On 'Nam... How education became indoctrination and what you can do about it*. That
title was a barrier to many people who saw it as just another
academic analysis by another Ph.D. My original goal was more
clearly stated in the subtitle: *Become a critical thinking decision
maker & advocate*.

PREFACE TO ORIGINAL EDITION

I had the privilege of being an assistant professor at a growing, dynamic community college in the Miami suburbs in the late '60s and early '70s. That institution has become one of the largest colleges in Florida with eight campuses,165,000 active students, and probably over a million graduates. The South Campus where I taught bears little physical resemblance to the core institution when I was on the faculty. It is an immense, architecturally attractive facility serving a vast diverse population.

As a military veteran, I had a skeptical view of the student deferments popular at the time and discovered that some students would register and pay but not actually attend classes. One student was honest enough to explain his rationale: The deferment was to avoid the draft and military service in an unpopular war in Vietnam. It was seen by many of the young men at the time to be a more acceptable option to pretending to be gay or running north to Canada.

Among the categories of college deferments that were granted by the US Selective Service, the clergy was a special category and teaching was a popular option.

The current appeal among university professors and their students for assailing capitalism and patriotism seems to have a common rationale. My hypothesis is that the men who chose to avoid serving in the military and elected instead to study to become teachers and preachers during the Vietnam conflict era have grown in seniority and influence. Their own lack of patriotic obligation or bias against serving their country in either the military or some similar civil service position carries over to their attitude and how they educate their students and influence their congregations.

That led me to the hypothesis I call "Blame it on 'Nam," and this book documents the change of mindset in faculty and demonstrates the result, which leads to a commonsense solution to remedy the consequences of that takeover of the US education system and many of our churches.

I provide an easy-to-implement program of calm, focused, community involvement and discussion that will improve social discourse and debate. From the family level to the leadership of our communities, my program can positively impact the curriculum and, thereby, the skills of the students.

Contents

CHAPTER 1

Introduction to the Argument

Why read this book?

Superior management always explains clearly to the affected group two key elements: why we are doing something different, and what is the objective, the goal; that is to say begin with the end in mind.

I wrote this book because I witnessed decisions being made by politicians and advisors at the highest levels of government that didn't appear to be based on facts, but more on projections, expectations, and often conflicting or incomplete models. I am convinced that different, more effective choices would have been made if the decision makers had applied some basic critical thinking skills. I have taught critical thinking skills for a decade to freshman college students and believe the investment in sharing those key questions would help people make better decisions in their daily lives. Sharing what I know to be effective questions is my contribution to that process.

This is not a politically oriented book. Some of the past legislation and regulations have been driven by political agendas and have impacted the education process. But the conclusion to incorporate critical thinking is not one based on ideology. Calm probing debate over how to resolve problems will vary. Individuals with a different concept of the role of government will most certainly see the solution choices differently. But that should be a matter of how best to use the data and implement choices, not in recognizing the cause or source of the challenge. Effective decisions must be based on verified data, not flawed models or projections, or worse, wishful thinking.

Parents and grandparents, teachers and counselors have a responsibility to teach children how to learn, not what to learn, and to provide them with appropriate tools to make individual decisions that will enable them to be productive, successful adults in whatever career they may choose. Coaches and mentors, civic and religious leaders all share that responsibility through demonstrating by example the rights and responsibilities of good citizenship.

The subsequent analyses and suggested solutions are intended to provide the reader with a set of concepts and issues that when applied consistently will result in decisions that have a potential for a positive impact on the lives of the decision makers and their community at large.

My goal is to create a cadre of advocates who are eager to challenge the local school boards or boards of regents that control the curriculum in the public education institutions in their community or state. The request is to restore the teaching of the rights and responsibilities of citizens, and to incorporate teaching critical thinking skills

My desire is for parents and teachers to practice by example from the early grades that we should be asking a half dozen or so questions of the sources of the information presented as facts. That will enable us to differentiate between opinions and facts, projections based on valid data and propaganda based on an ideology, and to carefully evaluate the expertise and reliability of the sources of the information being presented.

Four levels of different readers

In developing the supporting materials for the training courses and seminars I have identified four levels of individuals who want to foster improvement in public education. Apprentice. Challenger. Advocate. Visionary.

Apprentice

I am confident that not all of you reading this will want to devote the time and energy to become advocates eager to engage public officials in repairing and reforming public education. Some may only want to learn the basic skills to become a respectful skeptic and build the habit of asking key questions of the massive volume of information that is presented to us daily and become an Apprentice. Become comfortable in evaluating critically the validity of the data, and the experience and record of reliability of the source.

Challenger

Someone who wants to expand on the basic skills and become a Challenger does their own research into the reputation and track record of those promoting a concept or ideology. An individual who wants to demonstrate by example within their own family and close circle of associates the ability to reason and discuss the probability that positive outcomes could result from implementing the proposal. Home school parents who want to develop useful skills in their children would likely be in this category.

Advocates

Individuals who are motivated to publicly debate education policy and want to go beyond the research and personal circle of influence to improve education. They evaluate the sources and assess the reliability of the authors and the models upon which they are basing their projections. Advocates are respectful skeptics eager to engage in productive public debate. They request evidence to support the ideas and programs being presented by the bureaucrats and political leaders who are making decisions that directly impact you and your family member's lives and livelihoods.

Advocates and visionaries will be comfortable approaching and discussing issues with high level bureaucrats and administrators armed with sound well thought out rationale for change and prepared to present the benefits to those who will be directly and indirectly impacted by the changes. They are individuals who are prepared and know the background and experience of the board members, and the rules and regulations of their region. Community members who are confident in public and politely but firmly and persistently make a focused, targeted short presentation with a clear call to action.

Visionaries

The final category I have identified are individuals who consistently apply critical thinking skills with a demonstrated record of management in growing organizations who have the experience of implementing effective change. Visionaries will have a larger circle of influence and contacts they can reach out to engage in productive private and public debate of the pros and cons of existing and proposed education materials. Respected men and women whose personal circles of influence include community leaders who share the concern and a desire to evaluate and improve the outcomes of public education programs.

Visionaries will have the time and resources to coordinate and encourage a team of Advocates in their state or region. They will need a solid understanding of how to build and implement the Action Plan with a firm grasp of the legal and contractual resources and requirements of their sphere of influence and be available to assist the Advocates in their region.

Visionaries will be resourceful and energetic and willing to engage in periodic retreat style settings with likeminded individuals to build a solid overarching community of advocates for a national Action Plan coordinated by state or region. I predict the need for 100 Visionaries. Why the number one hundred? There are 50 states and two Visionaries per state would be one goal. Also, there are 94 US District Courts in the United States and the territories, sometimes two or three districts within a single state. I believe some of the most impactful change will only occur with court debate and approval. Some districts are very large, complex bureaucracies. For example, the Southern District of New York and Central District of California for example, are the largest by number of judges, with 28 judges each.

Follow through

After you've read this book, I invite you to join other members of what I believe will become a community focused on improving the quality of our public schools. Please become active in our Facebook and Linked In groups and share your goals and achievements. And yes, share your frustrations too, as there are likely to be others who have faced similar objections and overcome the resistance. Individually we have little chance to overcome the entrenched bureaucracy, but in significant numbers, we will prevail and our children and grandchildren will be empowered when we do.

A Teacher's Guide

As a former professor and adult trainer, I know how useful it is to have a resource available that helps to allocate the time available in a class. To assist the teachers and homeschool moms and dads, I have created a separate focused Guide to provide the outline of a lesson plan including a self-evaluation of the effectiveness of that plan.

The Teacher's Guide provides a worksheet for each class with notes and reminders on how to utilize the basic questions with each text or article that is being covered in that lesson. Included is a series of twenty-six worksheet pages for a two-semester schedule, teacher's notes for implementation, and time to be allocated of the class to the CT aspects. They are two-sided pages with open spaces for teacher's notes. The first page is a Teacher Planning Page. It includes:

- Topic for the day.
- The author and their credentials.
- Why this is valuable for the student to understand and how it applies to them.
- How the teacher will develop and approach the subject: Lecture / Q&A / summary with exercises to practice application and demonstrate understanding.

I believe the Guide will enable teachers and parents who share the responsibility of getting the young minds in their care into the habit of asking key questions to become productive adults who make decisions based on facts.

The Guide is available on Amazon at a low cost.

An analogy to consider

Imagine you just bought a new electric car. You used the last of your savings for a modest down payment and borrowed most of the money to have the latest model and favorite technological advances to be in vogue with all your successful friends. Soon after you drive it off the dealer's lot, you discover there are only a limited number of places to recharge the battery and you can't really drive more than fifty miles from home. Then to add insult to injury, the battery proves defective, and it won't hold a charge for more than a few hours.

Would you just shrug your shoulders or go and demand a refund or replacement? Or if that wasn't productive, go stand in front of the dealer with a sign to protest? Or maybe go find a sympathetic young lawyer eager to make a statement who agrees to file a lawsuit challenging the dealer's claims of reliability and serviceability?

Now substitute "college degree" for "electric car" and add into the mix that the lender's political friends have closed your place of employment and you've lost your source of income and have to move back home.

Would you sit idly by? Probably not. First, you would be all over social media with your sad story of the unfair outcome and soon discover thousands of cohorts are in the same situation. Now you and your social media friends can quickly mobilize a large crowd to protest in front of the dealership demanding reparations and compensation and a new car.

Why are there not thousands of recent college graduates protesting in front of Congress or the deans' offices at their universities instead of marching in the streets of their local communities to protest other issues? Much like a defective battery in an electric car, they have essentially gone into debt to buy a product—a college degree—that isn't helping them get where they want to go.

How could thousands of young people be marshalled and motivated in hours to pile into the streets of a dozen major cities and wreak havoc on the citizenry, and especially the police, with whom the majority of the marchers have never had an encounter—positive or negative? How could they possibly think that it is acceptable behavior for a small, angry subset of the protestors to break the windows of the storefronts and loot the contents over some other individual's perceived injustice?

The answer, I believe, is rooted in events that took place long before these eighteen- to twenty-five-year-olds were alive, thus the title of the original exposition, *Blame it on 'Nam.*

I believe the answer is deeply rooted in the failure of the public education system in the United States.

In the following chapters, I will establish the links and chain of events and key legislation that was imposed and implemented starting in the 1960s, ostensibly to improve public education. These changes have done little to affect a better educated public. Certainly, they have not produced a public that has any sense of history or civics, or the ability to use critical thinking skills.

You will see documentation of the results of those changes in the curriculum, the turnover and replacement of faculty, and the lowered performance of the graduates of high schools and colleges. Experienced educators have disclosed the inside stories of their experiences, so you will become aware of the self-selection process by which faculty at schools and colleges are hired and how the evaluation process of the effectiveness of the faculty bears little relationship to the skill levels achieved by their students.

More importantly, you will be provided with an action plan, a process to harness your frustration, and the tools to have a direct impact on improving the outcomes and correcting the mismanagement of the education system. You can do this though personal action and involvement at the local community level to demand the addition of just one course to the curriculum. This course will provide the students and their cohorts, family, and neighbors with the tools to sort fact from propaganda, education from indoctrination, and make rational, logical, well-developed arguments for appropriate change.

If you are up to the challenge, join me for the tour. I promise it will be eye-opening and, best of all, provide you with a foundation to improve your life and the lives of those you care about. The concepts you will discover will impact your daily life. You will learn the techniques and how to apply the crucial skills of a critical thinker and if you use those skills in your everyday decisions, you increase the opportunity for successful results. We all make choices daily. What to eat. Where to go and what to do. Where to work and where to live. Choices that are often unconscious and sometimes the results are positive, sometimes not. Each of those choices are what businesspeople call decisions. Decisions have consequences. If we develop the habit of carefully analyzing and verifying the information upon which we base those choices, the decisions are more likely to have positive impact. Applying critical thinking to decision making and carefully evaluating the information upon which we make those daily individual decisions is essential for successful outcomes in business and society at large.

The Argument

The core argument is that there is a problem in the knowledge and capabilities of graduates of US universities and colleges. Answers to simple questions posed to many recent graduates about important topics leave their parents aghast that their sons and daughters do not know the answers.

Graduates of Ivy League schools simply shrug their shoulders when they do not know that there are three separate but equal branches of US governance, or much about history, as if it isn't important. That lack of knowledge is perceived by the senior generations as unacceptable and they believe it leads the younger generations to making inappropriate choices.

What's Missing?

One thing many students lack is the ability to solve problems. This skill has several sets of proven procedures that usually begin with identifying the problem, researching probable causes of the problem, determining options to modify or change the circumstances that created the problem, then selecting the perceived best option and implementing that choice. Effective problem solving requires follow-up and continual evaluation of the efficacy of the implemented choice is necessary to determine if the problem has been resolved, or has it been merely modified or morphed into a different problem.

The concept of critical thinking is also missing from our collective curriculum. Philosophers have debated the benefits of critical thinking as an educational goal since the early 1900s and the topic is brought up in the writings of John Dewey, who called it reflective thinking. For our purposes I describe it as the habit of persistent analysis of information sources and evaluation of competing arguments—pro or con—of an issue. The goal, of course, is to determine which sources provide the most accurate, complete, and unbiased summary of the facts so that a thoughtful person can make an intelligent choice of which to accept and to base their decisions on the best evidence available. Students at critical levels of their education are not exposed to the concepts that might lead them to intellectually challenge the material and opinions of their teachers and preachers that are being presented as fact.

I discuss the goal of improving education by including critical thinking courses and the process of thoughtful analyses and the benefits that flow from that. This book begins with defining the problem, then in the process of researching probable causes applies many of the "right questions," including looking at potential value conflicts and assumptions, evaluating the evidence, looking for possible rival causes, evaluating if any of the statistics are deceptive, and what other reasonable conclusions are possible.

Generational Change

Another element to consider is the common issues of generational change. The influences that affect the attitudes and positions of each successive generation is an area of study that has been extensively written about by sociologists. It is a serious influence, and you will be exposed to some key insights developed in their analyses. Each generation seeks to modify their behavior to offset or overcome the perceived flaws and failures of their parents.

Influence of Government

Standing front and center of the issue are both legal requirements and negotiated agreements. The influence of government regulations on the changes in curriculum, at both the preparatory levels and the impact on subsequent acceptance at the university level, are dramatic. There are many university insiders who argue the hordes of administrators required to manage all these state and federal rules, who now occupy more office space on university campuses than teaching faculty, are a large reason for the increase in costs of tuition. The costs to monitor and manage the education rules are only part of the problem. Another significant impact on the process and resulting outcomes of education is the impact of negotiated agreements between state and local school boards and the faculty and their representatives. In the largest US school districts, those contracts are hundreds of pages long, detailing the rights and requirements of the government with respect to the faculty, but with little or no requirements for accountability based on outcomes.

Cost versus Benefit of the Investment?

The government also influenced the financial aspects of university attendance by changing the way that university education is paid for, which cannot be ignored either. Included in the analyses is the impact on the perceived value of a college diploma depending on the focus of the graduate's major and the possible influence of too easily available financing on decisions about what to study. The economic realities are not faced or fully realized until entering the work force. Some insiders have exposed the economics and it leads to questions about whether the encouragement to pursue an education and a degree in a program of study that has a high price, but limited market opportunities, could be considered a violation of fair practices or even rise to the operation of a criminal enterprise.

Curriculum Changes

Central to the proposed solution is that citizens at the local and state levels aggressively demand a change to the curriculum at the K–12 and university levels for the inclusion of critical thinking. Several authors' ideas on that topic are provided, which can be recommended as a starting point. Critical thinking courses should be introduced in middle school and then reinforced at the sophomore level in high school and freshman introductory courses at the university.

Community Involvement

Community groups need to be organized to discuss and assess if these topics are being fairly presented to their students and, if not, how to encourage and/or demand that the information critical to becoming a thoughtful individual is implemented. Once a proposed solution is selected, there is a need to deal with the psychological barriers to change. We will present some successful ways to implement significant change, how to effectively deal with the challenges, and overcome the innate resistance to change.

It will take a committed cadre of local-level individuals in small groups to advocate and press for the changes that are needed. The slow takeover of education did not occur overnight. It took almost two generations while the public sat by quietly, assuming that professional educators were trained and motivated to a higher level. That has been shown to be a false premise.

It may even require some persuasive legal arguments to overcome the resistance to the redesign and refocus of public education. Perhaps among the arguments for change should be consideration of legal challenges to the boards of education and boards of regents. Nearly all states' regulations preclude the use of classrooms for the presentation of political purposes.

If it can be shown that faculty and the administrations have clearly violated the rules established for managing education, then legal action may be warranted. It may take a class action lawsuit or two of key university administrators to get their attention, but surely there are some lawyers who share our concerns and would be willing to provide those professional services and challenge the status quo in education.

CHAPTER 2

Why Bother?

*T*he first question to address when confronting a perceived problem is to determine if it is worth the trouble to diagnose, analyze, and sort through potential solutions and then, with some luck and persistence, implement a successful remedy.

The goal of this book is to convince the reader that the key element that is not being adequately taught in our public institutions of learning, or being absorbed by the students, is to develop the skill of thinking critically. Another goal is to encourage the reader to become an active advocate for better and more broad-based presentation of critical thinking skills in our public education systems at multiple levels.

We need to start early in a child's development, in the seventh grade, to be sure to provide the students with an introduction to the concept before some of them may elect to drop out after the eighth grade, the first point when there is an option to step out of compulsory public school education in many states. A more serious discussion and practice is needed at the sophomore level in high school.

Most importantly, we need a serious in-depth course in critical thinking for first-year university and community college students. They are going to be exposed to a variety of research publications, white papers, and professorial viewpoints and need to develop the intellectual skills to separate fact from fiction and promotion from propaganda. These students need to be prepared to engage in spirited, but polite, debate of the issues, and to make informed, thoughtful decisions. My goal is not to convince students to conclude a certain way but to come to their conclusions after careful consideration of the facts and circumstances they face and to make a reasoned projection of potential consequences of their choices.

Why critical thinking skills?

Critical thinking enables an individual or group to make better informed choices. To begin, we will explore the main elements of critical thinking before we embark on the adventure to determine the likely causes that resulted in this skill not being applied more often than it appears to be by people in their personal lives or by their political decision makers.

Selecting from the wide range of information sources available and determining which sources are providing accurate and unbiased data is a crucial first step. In today's information age, there are literally hundreds of sources of data available at the touch of button on a handheld device on a wide range of topics. We need to educate the user/consumer to be selective in what they accept and react to.

Steven D. Brookfield is an educator and scholar in adult education and has written several books on how to develop critical thinkers and how to teach critical thinking. He identified four main components of critical thinking:

- Identifying and challenging assumptions
- Challenging the importance of context
- Imagining and exploring alternatives
- Using the exploration of alternatives to be reflective and skeptical.[1]

His books are high-level texts and suitable for university level and adult education. I have used them at both the freshman and graduate course levels with some success.

Chuck Clayton is an experienced mechanical engineer and business problem solver who wrote an easy-to-comprehend guide to critical thinking titled *The Re-Discovery of Common Sense! A Guide to: The Lost Art of Critical Thinking.*[2] He argues that if a logical stream is followed, then the decision and subsequent action is likely to be positive. He identifies several key elements in sequence, starting with thinking through the issues; gathering facts and data; then considering the assumptions and risks. He urges that a decision maker needs to analyze issues from multiple viewpoints and to do the necessary investigation to validate the information being used in the decision process.

Almost as important as what to do, Clayton presents a short list of barriers to critical thinking, which he calls *landmines*. They include egocentric thinking, social conditioning, biased experience, arrogance and intolerance, and two items most of us can identify with: a lack of time and patience. He further explains the problem with groupthink and the condition often called herd mentality. In addition, he warns his readers of the risk of a drone mentality, which is merely moving through life and barely observing what is going on around you without being engaged and involved.

My freshmen students have found his material engaging and informative. As a professor, that is a crucial first step in getting the students to absorb and apply what they are studying. In preparing my freshman students to be able to do basic research for a report or presentation, I used an integrated summary based on both Brookfield and Clayton to develop the "why" the topic was important using current examples of issues in the news to encourage them to consider what was going on around them in a more comprehensive way.

Key habits to become a critical thinker.

I then assigned a more detailed reading in another book by M. Browne and Stuart M. Keeley,[3] which provides a list of eleven questions to be used in being a critical thinker. I began teaching that course in 2010 using Browne and Keeley's eighth edition. Their book is now in the eleventh global edition, so it clearly has staying power. The course I was teaching is one of the first that international students take, so we focused on a subset of the questions with a slight modification as it applied to investigating and recommending actions to current topics of interest in their community and region of the world.

Many international students had not been exposed to any basic statistics or other analytical skills beyond the general math required of high school seniors. The concepts of statistical significance or relevance and impact of "selective data selection" was unfamiliar to them. Many of those students had never considered that news programs or newspapers had a political agenda. The feedback provided was they appreciated being exposed to the issues of critical thinking.

We will discuss more of the steps Browne and Keeley recommend in detail in the implementation section, but the conceptual material could be easily absorbed by seventh or eighth grade students. It can provide them with the basic understanding of the problems that can result if they merely accept information without any inquiry as to the knowledge or skill level of the source or potential agenda or bias of the information sources.

In a *New York Times* story by Lane Wallace from 2010,[4] Roger Martin, the then new dean of the Rotman School of Management in Toronto, had an encounter that led him to the conclusion that business school education needed to be more than finance and marketing. Specifically, he determined that students needed to learn how to approach problems from many perspectives and to combine various approaches to find innovative solutions. The article cites examples of Rotman graduates demonstrating integrative problem discovery and solving by using Martin's introductory course skills, "Fundamentals of Integrative Thinking," where the students are encouraged and trained to break decision models down to the core assumptions and logic.

Many other business programs, especially at the MBA level, have slowly integrated these concepts, but it is not uniform across the university programs, both private and public. It is incumbent on the student and the parents paying for their education to evaluate the coursework of the program and the reputation of its faculty for an even and fair inclusion of diverse perspectives in the coursework they will be studying.

If you agree with me that there is both a problem and a solution to be gained by an addition to the courses of study, then you will want to continue to read this book. You will be armed with the tools and supporting data to engage in an informed dialogue with your children, your neighbors, and your elected school board officials. You will be more persuasive in arguing for effective change that will enhance your life, your family's experience, and have a net positive impact on your community.

CHAPTER 3

What Happened?

A s a result of several factors in 2020, most notably the global pandemic, the world is in the midst of a series of social crises. Politicians are making decisions that have altered the way most of the world lives or dies. Individual liberty is restricted. International travel is difficult. The world economy has contracted, significantly decreasing resources available to governments and individuals alike.

In consideration of how important these changes and decisions are, how could it be that only a mere handful of journalists and news editors even considered asking any serious questions of the information or the sources of that information used as a basis for the decisions being made? Why aren't more people in media using critical thinking skills?

How could it be that reaction to the current failures at nearly all levels of government—uninformed individuals making political choices based on incomplete models—and almost nobody bothered to ask critical questions about the statistics or model makers, or the agendas and history of the so-called experts?

How could it be that the citizens across the globe are willing to sit by and quietly comply with arbitrary rules and regulations that are in clear conflict with long accepted standards of personal liberty and equitable treatment?

Vietnam War Influence on Enrollment

My argument is that the high school and university education curriculum has failed to provide a useful educational base for a significant portion of the cohorts of students they have had on campus for the past two or three decades. I believe that the curriculum was heavily influenced by thousands of individuals who preferred not to serve in the military and fight an ill-conceived war halfway around the world in the rice paddies of Vietnam. To avoid being drafted, many chose to pursue educational opportunities that provided legitimate avoidance of serving by self-selecting to become teachers or members of the clergy.

I was an assistant professor in the late 1960s and an active reservist after serving four years active duty. At the age of nineteen, I was a USAF physiological training technician, graduated US Army Special Forces Airborne School, and had jungle combat and survival training to be better qualified to teach pilots and crew members how to bail out of a disabled aircraft and survive once they got on the ground. I subsequently served as a loadmaster on the then aging C-119 aircraft and interacted weekly with Army Airborne trainees from Fort Bragg. As a Vietnam-era vet, to say I was skeptical of college deferments for young men who were not really attending courses would be an understatement. It helped form my working title: *Blame It on 'Nam.*

My arguments are also based on more recent experience as an adjunct professor at an overseas campus of a respected US-based university. I've had almost a decade of teaching the sons and daughters of financially successful parents; all graduates of expensive private education institutions, preparing themselves to go the states. Despite this education, many students demonstrated only a vague knowledge of the history of their own country, never mind what happened in other countries. More telling was they readily admitted to getting their news almost exclusively from social media sources. Until they were exposed to the core issues of critical thinking, it had not occurred to them to question whether what was presented as fact had really happened.

My personal anecdotal experience is supported by some more substantiated research by respected academics.

David Card and Thomas Lemieux published an academic analysis of the differences between men and women who entered college and university environments in the 1960s.[5] They found a statistically significant increase in men who were born from 1942 to 1950 in college attendance in the late '60s. That increase led them to estimate that draft avoidance raised college enrollment by 4–6 percent over what would be expected. They also argue that the change to a lottery draft in 1969 explains in part the decline in new draft deferments for college attendance, as young men were no longer at risk for the wider age range from nineteen to twenty-five, but only for one year. The risk of actually being drafted was changed and selection was the result of a random draw based on a combination of month and day of birthdate.

In 1992, *The Washington Post* published an opinion article, "Avoidance and the Draft,"[6] with a commentary on a previous story by Jim Fallows. John C. Fletcher, a professor of biomedical ethics and religious studies at the University of Virginia reported on a study he did for the Lilly Endowment on the enrollment in all Protestant seminaries that reported to the Association of Theological Schools between 1960 and 1980. Enrollments increased 31 percent from 1966 to 1971, compared to just 3 percent from 1960 to 1966. His memories of teaching were that many men who would have pursued other educational goals had what he termed a "gold standard" deferment by entering a theological school. The formal end of the draft was Dec 31, 1972.

Impact of the Draft

Amy Rutenberg published an article in 2013 describing the impact of the Vietnam draft on civilian occupations and domestic arrangements that were defined as in the national interest. Later, when she was an assistant professor of history at Iowa State University, her perspective was also published as a *New York Times* editorial in October 2017 entitled "How the Draft Reshaped America."[7] The leadership of the Selective Service from WWII to Korea, General Lewis B. Hershey, believed that all men between eighteen and twenty-five—and the country itself— benefited from providing two years of military service. Rutenberg believed that Hershey shaped the Selective Service into a respected institution and while most men may not have wanted to dedicate two years to active military service, draftees generally complied.

Her perspective continues that the Kennedy-Johnson administration and the Cold War mentality of defeating the Soviet Union and Communism had a direct impact on the way the

Selective Service operated with the cooperation of the secre-taries of defense and labor, working together to increase the inclusion of otherwise "unqualified" candidates. Those men were largely from poor underserved communities with lower educational skills. The Department of Defense (DOD) under Secretary McNamara actively wanted the armed forces to be a part of the solution to "rehabilitate" men caught in a cycle of poverty and advocated that military service could break that cycle and increase the skills of men.

Rutenberg claims McNamara believed that this policy would improve national security by reducing social unrest and benefit the American combat readiness by boosting the number of men in uniform. In August 1966, the DOD announced a program intended to bring 100,000 previously ineligible men into the mil-itary each year and these so-called "New Standards" men were to be admitted to all branches of the services either voluntarily or by the draft. Between 1966 and 1971, 354,000 of these men were added to the armed forces. According to Rutenberg, 40 percent of them were black, at a time when African Americans made up only 9 percent of the armed forces and about that percentage of the overall US population.

When the Cold War was the issue, most middle-class men did not see a need or benefit for military training to help them. They had more resources and those who were college students, teachers, or scientists got deferments. When the war got hot, many in that cohort figured out ways to avoid service.

Benefits of Enlistment

The most effective way to avoid being drafted into the infantry was to enlist and choose the branch of service, select the training regimen, and, to some extent, the timing of entering the service. Before the lottery, temporary deferments for college study and even graduate school pushed the timing forward. If you went to graduate school and studied law, medicine, dentistry, and even veterinary medicine, the military would defer your entry into the service and give you a direct commission as an officer. Some chose to join the Reserves or the National Guard, but there were long waiting lists for those.

A side benefit for those who did serve was the availability of the GI Bill to provide support and enable them to attend educational programs after military service. The monthly stipend in the early 1970s was a mere $220 for a single veteran—equivalent to about $1,000 a month in 2001 dollars. But, I can attest that it almost paid a month's rent at the time.

In a *Washington Post* February 1992 opinion piece, Roger Brooks, a Cambridge, Massachusetts, native and Harvard graduate with a master's degree in international law, objected to Fallows' argument about how he and his classmates avoided the draft. Brooks argued, "Because of the way in which Jim Fallows, Gov. Clinton and others reacted to the possibility of being drafted and called to active duty, that America's elite universities came to be perceived by the general public as isolated bastions of elitism...."

I believe there is ample documented evidence to support my observation that Vietnam had a major impact on who studied what and that those men went on the become the faculty at colleges, universities, and K–12 schools, thus validating my proposition that the teachers and preachers of that era have had a profound effect on the students who passed through their classrooms. It is the lack of "patriotism" and the attitudes of the teachers who chose not to serve that appears to have affected the content of their courses. And thereby, the knowledge of history and governance obtained by their students.

Lack of Knowledge of History and Civics

For example, a study by the Annenberg Public Policy Center in September 2017 revealed that a significant portion of the US population had little knowledge of how the US government is organized or its history. Among the results was the concerning failure of a third of the Americans surveyed failed to name a single First Amendment freedom. Just 26 percent of respondents could name all three branches of government, and 33 percent could not name one. The study goes on with other examples, but the point is the results revealed that knowledge is skewed and heavily weighted by the age of the respondents. Of the people sixty-five and over, 74 percent passed, but only 19 percent under forty-five passed the test.

This study indicates there is a significant difference in what is known by different generations of students. The danger is evident on the front pages of our current newspapers. It is the middle-aged folks who do not know, or apparently care, about the rights and responsibility of citizens and lawmakers who are literally making life-and-death decisions.

Pandemic Decision Making

Just look at the pandemic. The consequences of the recent political decisions to address a health crisis have bankrupted hundreds of thousands of small businesses worldwide and impoverished the entrepreneurs and their employees with little economic justification for the government's cavalier decisions. Mandates were made to immediately cease operations and confine the potential consumers to their homes in what is becoming obvious overkill. Yes, the Wuhan virus is very contagious and spreads more rapidly than most previously encountered similar chemical agents. But, the evidence was there a month into the problem, had anyone bothered to look closely at the high infection rates versus death rates. it was clear that a small segment of the population had a very high risk, but the vast majority of the world population did not.

The high-risk population is over sixty with any underlying medical issues that adversely affected their overall health, especially their immune systems, such as diabetes and the often-interrelated obesity, lung congestion, or heart issues. Those people were at serious risk of becoming dangerously ill and dying if they contracted the virus. Those people needed to be isolated, closely monitored, and protected.

But that is not what happened, certainly not in the US. Children, especially, are barely at risk if they are otherwise healthy. Yet they have been denied access to school facilities and deprived of a year of schooling and integration with their peers, driven largely by fears of the middle-aged faculty and administrators.

At least half of the deaths in the worst center of the disease, New York City, were elderly individuals housed in nursing homes or extended care facilities. Facilities that were well known to the community health organizations to have been problematic in their resident-guest management and health protocols long before this pandemic swept around the globe. The only previous outside monitoring that seems to have been effective were visits by loved ones who were alerted to dangerous situations such as elder abuse, maltreatment, and malnutrition of the elderly residents. Through their own efforts, they pressured the facility management and sometimes local authorities to correct the misbehavior of unskilled and often unmotivated staff.

The recent COVID-19 political decisions prevented relatives from visiting and, ignoring for the moment, the detrimental psychological effect on both the isolated elderly and their younger family members from the enforced separation, no one was taking stock of how the residents were being treated and cared for. Inspections and consultations by health authorities on how best to protect the elderly residents were spotty and inconsistent.

This is not meant as a sweeping indictment of health care providers for the elderly, but rather a failure of the health monitoring systems generally under the oversight and funding of local government authorities who restricted access and thereby amplified the risks to the residents.

Are We Hearing the Truth?

Health workers who sounded an alarm and used social media to argue that the protocols put in place were inadequate, ill-informed, or simply not the way to behave, were systematically shouted down—or worse—silenced by the media technocrats who removed any conversations that were not in sync with pronouncements of the World Health Organization (WHO).

Even after the WHO was exposed as being ill-informed at best, or complicit at worst, in echoing the misinformation emanating from the source of the deadly virus, Wuhan, China, and the testing laboratory there, the restrictions and protocols continued. Early in the release of the deadly virus, the lone physician in China who sounded the alarm was silenced, "disappeared," and was thought to be in confinement in some remote re-education center or dead. It has recently been reported that he caught the virus and died due to it.

I believe the fault lies less in the political agenda of the journalists and editors, and instead lies in the lack of a well-balanced education of most Americans to include history, law and ethics, and analytical decision-making skills. Politicians and community leaders who have influence without the benefit of appropriate decision-making skills have been elevated to levels of leadership in universities and public education at the K–12 level. Many have gone into politics and have benefited enormously in technology enterprises.

I am more than willing to attribute their mistakes in judgment to a lack of critical thinking, not malevolence or intentional miscommunication. But that takes me back full circle to my original premise, *Blame it on 'Nam,* and the effect of those missing educational components that affected their perception and understanding of the world and how it works. Those educationally shortchanged offspring of the Baby Boomer generation, who were taught and matured in the '70s and '80s, rejected the classic core curriculum and are now the individuals who are in influential positions making decisions without asking the right questions.

Illiberalism Defined

I am not a lone voice who believes there is a problem. Robert P. George is the chaired professor of jurisprudence and director of the James Madison Program in American Ideals and Institutions at Princeton University and a frequent visiting professor at Harvard Law School. He argues that the core obligation of any liberal arts program is the pursuit, preservation, and transmission of knowledge. He believes that the politicization of the academy and the feeder schools has created "illiberalism." He describes this as "the unwillingness of so many members of college and university communities to entertain, or even listen to arguments that challenge the opinions they hold, whether those opinions have to do with climate science, racial or ethnic preferences, abortion, welfare policy, sexual morality, immigration, US foreign policy, the international economic order, or the origins of human consciousness."[8]

The investigation of the evolution of education includes generational issues. Sociologists have studied and carefully identified the shifts in behavior and personality of successive generations. Frequently, the younger generations strive to amend or correct perceived errors of their elders. That pattern of behavior has been well documented and is part of the explanation, but not all of it.

The less than positive outcomes in society are not just the result of flawed political decisions. You will discover it is a combination of legislation with unintended consequences, negotiated agreements between state and local school boards and the faculty, in addition to a lack of diversity in the perspectives of the decision makers. It isn't just flawed decision models that were poorly implemented and badly monitored.

In the following sections, you will see documentation of the change in outcomes and the perceptions of the value of a university education. You will learn the explanations of experienced, respected educators who pull back the curtain on the selection and promotion of the faculty and management at key universities. And we will review the work of respected sociologists who have identified the trends of successive generations and their focus. I believe the combination has dramatically altered the decision-making processes at the family, community, and national levels, and the resulting outcomes.

You will have an opportunity to decide for yourself if there is any correlation between these aspects and, if so, the subsequent section will be of interest in what we can do to remedy the decline in educational outcomes.

CHAPTER 4

Is There a Problem?

Perception versus Reality

The worldwide reputation for the value of a US university education has remained high. A 2020 ranking has seven of the top
ten universities in the world from the US: California Institute of
Technology (2), Stanford University (4), Massachusetts Institute
of Technology (5), Princeton University (6), Harvard University
(7), Yale University (8), and The University of Chicago (9). But
the survey is based in part on research and physical facilities,
endowments, and in part by the presence of many middle-aged
graduates in high profile positions in business and industry
and government positions. In other words, the reputation of
perceived value.

Marketing experts know that perception is more powerful
than reality, but a careful analysis of the skills of the graduates could lead to a different conclusion. It is more relevant to

compare the skills sets of the graduates than the number of graduates.

There are large numbers of college graduates who cannot find employment in a booming economy in a field related to their chosen degree. And five years after graduation, many are working in fields unrelated to the degree they obtained. That is a reality check on at least one level.

On another level is evidence that the students at these respected universities know little about the world in which they live and must function, which is disconcerting to say the least. Students and recent graduates of Ivy League schools cannot correctly answer basic questions about the process of governance, US history, or correctly identify past or current influential leaders. That lack of knowledge is perceived by older generations as unacceptable.

Evidence of the Decline in Skill Levels

We have more quantitative measures of the graduates of high school. Two common methods of evaluating the successful outcomes of high school educational experiences of the students are to compare graduation rates and entrance exam scores of those graduates who seek to go on to higher education.

According to the National Center for Education Statistics (NCES), average Scholastic Aptitude Test (SAT) scores in 1967 on verbal/critical reading was 543 and math scores averaged 516. SAT scores have steadily declined from 1972, as evidenced by the 1972 average math (509) and critical reading (530), through to 1980 when math dropped 17 points and reading scores dropped 28 points. The scores remained flat though the nineties and math scores recovered 15 points between 1990 and 2010. Critical reading scores remained flat and have since declined slightly more between 2000 (505) and 2016 (494). A good overview is available on the website_https://www.erikthered.com/tutor/sat-act-history.html.

Are the Underlying Issues Real?

The summer of 2020 brought thousands of largely young people out to the streets to protest the death of George Floyd in custody of a police officer and other similar incidents. How could it be that no one seemed interested in what happened in the five minutes preceding Mr. Floyd being pressed facedown in the street? How could it be that few of the protestors questioned those politically motivated individuals and groups that claimed false narratives as truths: Claims that motivated thousands of young people who flooded the streets to protest and confront the police?

Few analysts have provided an accurate perspective of the facts. Federal law enforcement statistics on arrests and confrontations between the public, both law-abiding and criminal, and the use of force are easily available online. Even the liberal newspaper *Washington Post* provided a summary of the relevant facts, but they were ignored. Why?

The response to the COVID-19 health issue exacerbated these protests in two ways. First, the student population was kept out of classrooms and therefore had nothing productive to do but chat on social media. News images were filled with video of students more interested in taking selfies and videos of their friends to document their participation in the unrest than considering the real issue of whether the death of a convicted felon was the result of excessive force or from a drug-induced reaction? Ignored by nearly everyone was the evidence that the victim, Mr. Floyd, was known to be a dangerous man by the lead officer involved and the autopsy later showed Floyd to be under the influence of drugs at the time of his arrest.

Impact of Black Lives Matter

More importantly, nobody asked for evidence of the "systemic violation of civil rights of blacks" being claimed by Black Lives Matter Foundation (BLM), an organization formed by three admitted Marxists who espouse a Communist agenda. Their foundation is an organization that was lavishly given millions in donations by celebrities and corporate marketing people. Money that has not been transparently accounted for or disclosed, to the dismay of some of the donors. Yet, few have even bothered to ask "show me the money," to quote a famous sports movie line.

The unwarranted, excessive use of force by police would be a worthy cause to protest. But, it provides yet another example of people who claim to be interested in improving the lives of their friends and neighbors, but who failed to look for the evidence of a real problem before they charge off on a crusade to vanquish a perceived victim or group.

So, yes. I believe there is evidence of a deeper problem. And the problem at its core is a lack of education in specific areas.

What Caused the Problem?

To make any serious attempt at a remedy for a problem, we need to determine the likely underlying cause or causes of the problem.

What follows for your analysis uses a widely accepted and proven business model for problem solving:

- Identify the problem
- Search for the likely causes
- Investigate potential solutions and rank them in order of potential success
- Select the most likely solution to impact and resolve the problem
- Implement that solution and monitor the progress

You will see evidence linking changes made in the education system under the federal leadership of what has traditionally been a local and state level responsibility: Determining the curriculum and course of study and the means to evaluate the outcomes. In a recommended solutions section, you will also learn how to successfully implement significant change.

There are several key variables that have influenced the outcomes of education. One is the centralization of the Federal Education Acts in 1965 and the half dozen changes since then. Another is the influence of contracts between the faculty and administration of public education. I believe that the education system currently being managed by the teachers and preachers of the past forty years are a key part of the problem. And there is the sociological change in attitudes and goals of successive generations.

Government Influence in Education

The earliest US public education systems were established in 1787 in what was then known as the Northwest Territories by the settlers who moved from New England and settled in what is now Ohio, Illinois, Michigan, Wisconsin, and part of Minnesota under the Northwest Ordinance. Led by conservative religious leaders of faith, who believed it was imperative that the young should be educated, they insisted that there be a requirement that land be reserved for the building of schools included in the Land Ordinance of 1785, which permitted the establishment of townships in the territory.[9]

Originally created in 1867 by then President Andrew Johnson, the first US Department of Education concept was to collect information and statistics about the nation's schools. It remained relatively small and operated under various agencies now falling under the US Department of Health and Human Services (DHHS). The current Department of Education has the role of federal oversight and has grown into a huge bureaucracy of over 4,000 employees with a budget of over $68 billion.

Starting in the 1960s a series of Federal Education Acts were signed into law. In 1965, then President Lyndon Johnson signed the Elementary and Secondary Education Act (ESEA) which put the federal government into the management role of K–12. It doubled the federal expenditures and changed the relationship between states and the central government. It was part of an effort to seek more balance in educational opportunities without regard to where students reside. US education is very decentralized, with states and regional boards of education specifically charged with determining what is to be taught in the schools in their area.

Since 1965, ESEA has been modified and reauthorized by Congress several times.[10] The Bilingual Education Act (BEA) provides support for bilingual education and educational efforts for Native Americans and other groups. The Equal Educational Opportunities Act (EEOA) of 1974 prohibits discrimination against students and teachers. The George Bush administration developed the No Child Left Behind Act (NCLB) in 2001 that introduced a testing regime designed to promote standards-based education; an attempt to drive national level outcomes. The Obama administration succeeded in getting Every Student Succeeds Act (ESSA) through Congress in 2015, which retained some of the testing requirements established by the NCLB, but shifted accountability provisions to the states.

The formal federal agency to oversee the country's educational system is only part of the equation. Congress and the department charged with implementing some of the more than twenty laws and provisions of the federal mandates regarding education have over 104,000 documents describing the policies and procedures to be followed. Many universities have more administrative staff on payroll to monitor compliance and implement the various rules and programs than there are faculty physically teaching in classrooms. The complexity and the staff needed to assure compliance is argued to be one of the reasons university tuition has outpaced the cost of living increases over the past two decades.

The cost of compliance is not the only aspect of federal rules. Another influence on the cost of education that must be included in the argument is the relative ease for students to obtain federal guaranteed loans to pursue their education. Universities do not have the usual constraints on cost containment of a regular for-profit business. Their customers have easy access to the funds to pay for their product or service. That eliminates the need for comparative shopping.

A summary of some relevant articles from as early as 1971 indicates this was a problem many saw as it was happening, yet no serious action to mediate the issue appears to have occurred.

In 1971, *Time* magazine ran the article "Education: Graduates and Jobs: A Grave New World," which stated that the supply of PhD students was 30 to 50 percent larger than the expected future demand in upcoming decades. In 1987, US Secretary of Education William Bennett suggested that the availability of loans may be fueling an increase in tuition prices and an education bubble. This "Bennett hypothesis" claims that readily available loans allow schools to increase tuition without regard to demand elasticity. College rankings are partially driven by spending levels and higher tuition is also correlated with increased public perceptions of prestige. Over the past thirty years, demand has increased as institutions improved facilities and provided more resources to students.

Some argue that such easily obtained money removes serious analyses of the cost versus benefits of what the students study and which degrees they pursue. Unfortunately, for many students, they discover that there is little perceived market value for what they have devoted the prior four—and often more like five years— studying. Added economic pressure from the fact that they graduate with a degree that has low income-generating value, the students are saddled with huge loan debt to be repaid from their earnings.

This combination adds at least two more problems for the student and society to be resolved. How do we prepare students to be able to evaluate options and to pursue an education with some reasonable expectation of employment and an economic return on their investment? And how to deal with the thousands of students who have a burdensome debt and are unprepared to repay it?

Is it any wonder that many recent graduates migrate to political candidates that promise a debt holiday and forgiveness of all their student loans? Student loans cannot be erased, even by legal filing for bankruptcy.

State and Local Contracts

University students may not be getting the educational outcomes the parents may expect, and probably think they have purchased in the form of tuition and related investment in their offspring's education. But the universities are working with the graduates of high schools and that is another layer of the problem.

In his book about charter schools,[11] Thomas Sowell summarized the challenges revealed by the former New York City Chancellor of Public Schools, Joel Klein, regarding the union contracts in major city school systems. The negotiated agreements of who can teach what, when, and for how much, is a big part of the shift in emphasis from education itself and the process to accomplish those learning goals to the protection of teachers' rights. The New York City teachers' union contract is said to run hundreds of pages long and governs minutia down to who can be assigned hall monitoring or lunchroom duties and who can't and, of course, the right to hold union activities during the school day. The California Education Code is reported to be over 2,500 pages.

Sowell's main argument is there in no accountability for educational outcomes in the public school system of New York City. Sowell provides a worrisome comparison of the differences in educational achievement as measured by the New York state examinations between students enrolled in a dozen charter schools and regular public schools. The students are drawn from the same neighborhoods and often taught in the same buildings as the public schools, yet the charter students on average accomplish a much more satisfactory outcome, especially among the poor inner city populations. As an advocate for charter schools, he provides an option which we will discuss further in the section on what we can do to improve.

I had the honor to be an assistant professor at a highly rated state university in the '80s and early '90s. As a state-funded university, it was required to accept any state high school graduate. The university devoted almost one-fourth of its undergraduate budget to remedial education. D. Patrick Saxon, PhD, and Hunter Boylan, PhD, respected authorities on developmental education, published an article[12] in the *Journal of Developmental Education* in 2001 wherein they reviewed five research studies into the cost of remedial education at the college level that were published in 1998 and 1999. The various studies of a range of individual states in the mid-1990s disclosed, for example, that Maryland spent $1.05 billion in the period 1993–94; Arkansas spent $27 million; City University of New York (CUNY) spent $124 million,

The Faculty Senate of CUNY argued that while that full-cost accounting may be accurate, which includes the fixed costs of classrooms and facilities and an allocation of the institution's administrative staff and overhead, the real cost was more like $30 million. But the study went on to reveal that remedial education was a cash flow source for many of these college programs and that the shift of the education from secondary school to the college level was less important than the training itself. The schools see it as an investment opportunity for the colleges rather than a weakness of the secondary schools. Their hypothesis was that in the long run, it reduced the likelihood of the students having to rely on social programs. Whether the taxpayers would agree or not does not seem to have been an item of academic interest.

The founder of the Khan Academy, an online not-for-profit organization formed in 2008, stated in a television interview that "remedial math" was a polite way of describing sixth and seventh grade mathematics.[13]

Salman Khan has created a financially successful enterprise, tuition free for students and teachers, that is supported by private donations in the millions from the likes of Carlos Slim and AT&T. His online academy has been successful in filling the gaps in acquired skills in math and reading for students and providing resources for teachers in multiple languages. In 2017, the Academy became an official partner with the College Board's Advanced Placement, the organization that administers the SAT.

This provides some insight in our desire to identify possible causes. Is the maze of state and federal regulations imposed on educational institutions and those who chose to become teachers and professors a possible reason for the falling ability of students to read critically or to solve mathematical problems as evidenced by the decline in SAT scores? Is it the result of community and state school boards constraining what is taught or how the student's performance is evaluated? Is it a shift in focus from the students' educational outcomes to teachers' rights?

Problem-solving models all depend on a realistic identification of the cause of the problem to be able to establish a plan to overcome, modify, or at least minimize the consequences.

Level of Motivation

This leads me to consider that the problem may not be the lack of interest or inability of students to learn, but perhaps a combination of lack of proper motivation on the part of parents and teachers. As a long-time faculty member at three different colleges and universities, I have observed that adult students who attend classes at night and on weekends are highly motivated to fill the gaps in what they didn't learn—or don't remember—when in high school or some of the core courses taken in their early years of general education at the university.

That experience suggests the multitude of regulations and procedures have diverted the teachers from their core mission: teaching and sharing knowledge in a way that excites the students and encourages them to actively participate in the process. Their focus instead has been diverted to meeting the paperwork demands of administrators and filling the check boxes on lesson plans, instead of focusing on the variety of students they face daily and the myriad of issues they bring to the classroom.

Even in respected universities, when faculty stray from the accepted dogma or political ideology, they risk demonization and harassment from the other faculty. There is also the issue of peer pressure on students and faculty to conform to the current social conditioning. One case in point is Professor William A. Jacobson, who teaches law at Cornell University. He made an argument that the organization behind the protests over the cases of Trayvon Martin and Michael Brown were being led by anti-American, anti-capitalist activists under the banner of Black Lives Matter. He has been subjected a smear campaign from other faculty, students, and even the dean of the law school who denounced him as a racist for even challenging the basis of the BLM argument. The professor described the culture on campus as one of zero tolerance; that political correctness has always been a factor on campus, but now, no criticism is tolerated.[14]

He explained that he is seen as out of step with what is fair and just and should be driven from the campus, which he attributed to the self-selection process of faculty hiring. If the new faculty appear to have conservative or traditional views on their resume, they are not likely to be interviewed or hired. He does not have tenure, but he felt secure that he would not lose his position on the faculty. He also revealed that there is silent support among many students who are intimidated to speak up on topics because of the personal costs to them from strident classmates and the risk of poor grades from activist professors that would hamper their graduation prospects and subsequent careers.

Biased Curriculum?

Is there biased history material being presented in K–12 classrooms in your neighborhood? There is currently a curriculum being adopted in classrooms in fifty states based on a project promoted by the *New York Times*. The "1619 Project" claims the US founders' primary motivation for separation from Great Britain was the protection of slavery. Many accomplished historians have cited facts and documents produced contemporaneously with the Revolutionary War that separated the colonies from the British Crown that demonstrate the "1619" argument to be inaccurate and incomplete. Were any of Jacobson's students taught this misinformation?

What can be done to revise or correct biased teaching or presentation of incomplete and incorrect material when it is done in a public school or college?

There is a potential legal aspect to the problem of what is being taught in our university classrooms. We will deal with a possible solution in more detail later. But the readers should be aware that in most states the charter authorizing public colleges and universities includes some specific language that was intended to prevent teachers from promoting a particular political perspective and from using their "captive audience" to propagandize. Professor John Ellis and others have pointed out that the deans and presidents of some of the largest university systems may be violating the mandates and regulations of the boards of regents, but to date have not been held to account for being compliant.

The usual argument from the faculty is they have "academic freedom" to present their material as they best deem appropriate. In fact, tenure has long been granted to insulate faculty from constraints on freedom of speech and from risk of presenting arguments opposed to current political opinion. If they have been granted tenure, they are almost impossible to dismiss or terminate.

The Case of Paul Sweezy

On the one hand, that is true. In 1957 the US Supreme Court overturned a New Hampshire ruling involving a university professor who was sentenced to jail for refusing to answer questions about university lectures he had given. Paul Sweezy was a Marxian economist who was challenged by the then Attorney General of New Hampshire, Louis Wyman, who was investigating Communist subversion in New Hampshire in 1953 under the state's Subversive Activities Act of 1951. Sweezy refused to answer questions about the content of his lectures or his links to Communism and whether he had advocated Marxism.

Chief Justice Earl Warren delivered the high court's ruling that the case was overly broad and that the New Hampshire Supreme Court exceeded the legislative intent. In a concurring opinion, Justice Frankfurter, a former professor at Harvard Law School, argued that institutions of higher learning were shielded from intervention by political authorities and that in both political arena and academic, thought and action are presumptively immune from inquisition by political authority.

The Sweezy case was lauded as an extension of the 1927 Brandeis court decision wherein Justice Brandeis defended free speech as follows:

"Citizens have an obligation to take part in the governing process, and they cannot do so unless they can discuss and criticize governmental policy fully and without fear. If the government can punish unpopular views, it cramps freedom, and in the long run, that will strangle democratic processes. Thus, free speech is not only an abstract virtue but also a key element at the heart of a democratic society."[15]

Faculty everywhere believe they are immune from challenges to expressing unpopular positions. The problem in the twenty-first century seems to be more that the faculty themselves are denying students the opportunity to be exposed to contrary, often conservative, voices or to exercise their rights of free speech when they are not in concert with the prevailing ideology on campus. In the case of the "1619 Project," students are being presented controversial and factually incorrect material without any evidence or discussion of the counter arguments.

The Other Side of the Issue

A curriculum called "1776 Unites"[16] was established by a long-standing, well-respected civil rights advocate, Robert L. Woodson, Sr., but has been slow to gain traction. President and founder of the Woodson Center, he has gathered a group of African American academics to promote entrepreneurship, self-determination, and mutual social support. Launched in February 2020 specifically to counter the "1619" arguments, there are seventeen essays pointing to historical positive contributions of black people throughout history.

I suspect it will take a class action lawsuit against one or two high profile university presidents and the boards of regents that oversee the program to bring some balance back into the opinions and perspectives which students are exposed to. Perhaps one of the readers is an attorney who would like to lead that charge?

Social Effects

Sophomoric: Defined in *Webster's* as "conceited and over-confident of knowledge but poorly informed and immature."

Sophomores are in their second year of high school or college. College sophomores are usually about eighteen or nineteen years old. A second-year college student in 2020 would have been born after the turn of the current century, members of a group sociologists call Millennials. According to many psychologists, people have no reliable personal recall of anything prior to being about five years old, so their "world experience" dates from 2005.

While there are no statistical analyses or accurate counts of the age and demographics of the 2020 protests over what most saw as an unjustifiable killing of an unarmed black man, television coverage shows mostly white college-aged men and women usually casually dressed and busy taking cellphone photos of themselves and their friends to document their participation. There were also ninja-clad armed protagonists who were enraged and violent.

Protest is justified over an injustice, but what is troubling is not just the violence that a small segment of the protestors engaged in (looting and burning innocent shop keepers' property). Where is the similar outrage over the gang violence that in one weekend in Chicago killed more young black people than the fourteen unarmed suspects that the Federal Bureau of Investigation (FBI) statistics report were shot by police in an entire year across the entire country?

That failure questions the organized protest promoters' argument that Black Lives Matter. Are the nearly all black 478 murder victims in Chicago in 2019 not important? Do their lives matter? Where is the outrage directed at the police and the political leadership in Chicago and other major cities over the carnage? Why weren't the protestors better informed?

Generational Differences

People change and form their world view as they mature. Their personalities develop around key events and this can create a collective narrative within a generation.

Sociologists have been studying generational behaviors for centuries. Most notable in the early development of the academic field of sociology was Talcott Parsons. Parsons studied biology, sociology, and philosophy as an undergraduate, then studied economics at the famed London School of Economics. He earned his PhD in sociology and economics at the University of Heidelberg in Germany where he met the organizational guru know by nearly all business management and MBA students, Max Weber, whose writings Parsons translated into English. Parsons joined the faculty at Harvard as an instructor of economics but was not comfortable in that academic climate. Instead, he moved to sociology and became the first chair of the newly formed Sociology Department in 1930.

Parsons spent time in Palo Alto, California, in the late 1950s and was influenced by anthropologists, writing a joint article with Alfred Kroeber, a Columbia PhD, in October 1958 titled "The Concept of Culture and the Social System."[17] In the student rebellion of the 1960s, Parsons' theory was criticized by some arguing it was too conservative. The politically left of the day even claimed that Parsons had been an opponent of the "New Deal." 26

Parsons' influential work, *Economy and Society*, was published in 1956. It is based on his development of a theory of symbolism in relation to action using a combination of Freud's theory and philosophy. A system he developed and massaged over his career is known as AGIL, which outlines four systematic core functions that are prerequisites for any society to be able to persist over time. They are Adaptation, Goal Attainment, Integration, and Latency.

Generational Archetypes

Parsons' work has been at the core of much of the development of sociology. Life Course Associates, a group organized on the teachings of William Strauss and Neil Howe in 1999, use descriptions of a four-phase model of social change devised by Parsons, who hypothesized that society moves into a new phase every time a demand for social order rises or falls.[18] Their work in the book, *Generations*, summarizes and expands on the age ranges and characteristics of generational names that have been in the public lexicon for decades, and are based on four characteristics: Prophet, Nomad, Hero, and Artist. The characteristics of each of these archetypes becomes important in our attempts to implement a change in behavior.

William Strauss and Neil Howe explain that the four archetypes repeat in series sequentially to cycles of what they call crises and awakenings, and that generations share not only age of birth in common but the same attitudes toward family, risk taking, culture, and civic engagement. They describe those archetypes as follows:[19]

Prophet: These individuals grow up as indulged children in a post-crisis era and come of age as self-absorbed crusaders who are focused on morals and principles in midlife, then emerge as elders into another crisis. Baby Boomers, sometimes called Boomers, are of this archetype.

Nomad: This generation enters childhood in times of social ideas and spiritual agendas that, as young adults, attack the established institutional order. They grew up as underprotected children, come of age alienated, but become pragmatic midlife leaders. Gen Xers are in this group.

Hero: This generation enters childhood at a time of pragmatism, self-reliance, and laissez-faire. They grow up as protected children, come of age as team-oriented optimists, emerge as energetic, overly confident midlifers, and age into politically powerful elders. Millennials are in the category.

Artist: This generation enters childhood during a crisis period when dangers cut down social and political complexity that results in aggressive institutions with an ethic of personal sacrifice. They grow up overprotected by adults and come of age as socialized, conformist young adults. They become process-oriented midlife leaders and age into thoughtful elders. Generation Z, aka "Homelanders," are in this category.

These cyclical generations, as defined by Strauss & Howe starting at the beginning of the twentieth century, are first named as GI (Hero, born 1901–1924), then Silent (Artist, born 1925–1942), Boom (Prophet, born 1943–1960), Generation X (Nomad, born 1961–1981), Millennial (Hero, born 1981–2004), and Homelander (Artist, born after 2005).

Projections and forecasts of sociologists based on these turnings include one very prophetic article published in *Futurist* magazine, July–August 1997 issue, by Strauss and Howe. The article, titled "Demography," predicted a two-decade era of crisis starting with some then as yet to be determined spark around 2005. They argued, accurately as it turned out, "that remnants of the existing social order would disintegrate, political and economic trust would implode, and real hardship will ensue."

How Generations Affect Each Other

What is the link between the Baby Boomer generation, the Gen Xers, and Millennials? To determine this, we need to look at what was the social focus of the 1970s. Early Baby Boomer generation members, born in the post-WWII decade, came of age in the 1960s and were at the center of "free love" and an "anything goes" environment. They promoted the Equal Rights Amendment (ERA). It was a time when women were burning their bras and their boyfriend's draft cards in protest. December 4, 1961 is heralded as a landmark day for women's rights; the date contraceptive pills became available, credited with sparking a sexual revolution. In 1965, we saw the first of several US Supreme Court decisions regarding the distribution of birth control. And in 1973, the famous Roe v. Wade decision struck down a Texas anti-abortion law, in effect legalizing the procedure. Roe was a generic name assigned to the real plaintiff and Wade was the District Attorney for Dallas County, where the real woman lived.

The Boomers were the principal age group of the protestors in the late-1960s. Strauss and Howe describe them as children who were raised with the parenting theories of Dr. Benjamin Spock, who advocated a gentler, more permissive style of parenting, and *Father Knows Best* complacency. For younger readers, that was a popular TV sitcom that portrayed the "typical American family" with a wise father and compliant wife and children, that ran from 1954 to 1960 and resembled a series of Norman Rockwell paintings popular in the same era. Even the youngest Boomers, born in 1960, are now of retirement age and comprise a reliable voting bloc. They were also among the group of those tested on civics and history that got most of the answers correct to what was a modified "citizenship test" mentioned in the previous chapter.

Generations Through American History

Among the questions that could be asked of Boomers is "Where were you in '72?"

That was the year of the re-election of President Richard Nixon. It was the first election after the voting age was lowered to eighteen, and a landslide victory over a Democrat opponent who argued for the end of the Vietnam War and the immediate guarantee of a minimum income. Nixon won 60.7 percent of the popular vote, with more than 18 million more votes than his opponent, and forty-nine of the states with a 520–17 electoral vote margin. His opponent, the former senator from South Dakota, George McGovern, carried just Massachusetts and the District of Columbia.

Nixon campaigned on his success in international diplomacy. His administration did end the Vietnam War with the signing of the Paris Peace Accords on January 27, 1973. The main negotiators of the agreement were United States National Security Advisor Henry Kissinger and North Vietnamese politburo member, Lê Đuc Tho. Those two men were awarded the 1973 Nobel Peace Prize for their efforts, although Lê Đuc Tho. refused to accept it.

Sophomores in 1968 were probably born in 1950, the year the Communist North Korean Army crossed the border, invading South Korea. The first US Army troops arrived on the first of July, after the North had captured the South's capital city, Seoul. These 1950s early memories of a child would begin about 1955, two years after an armistice agreement was signed, pausing the conflict in Korea.

The children of the 1950s were educated mostly by women and a few men. Those adults had been raised during the Great Depression, served in and survived World War II and the Korean Conflict, and were experiencing the economic growth of postwar boom. The Veterans Administration (VA) guaranteed home mortgages for veterans encourage family home ownership, and most experienced the personal satisfaction of being what was later anointed the title of *The Greatest Generation*, a book written by retired newsman, Tom Brokaw.

Children born in 1950 would have been about twelve years old when then President John F. Kennedy (JFK) was assassinated in Dallas, Texas on November 22, 1963. His Vice President, former Texas senator and skilled politician, Lyndon B. Johnson (LBJ), assumed the presidency. This was a role he had campaigned for but came in second at the Democratic Convention to JFK, who then asked him to be his running mate. On a personal note, I was serving in the USAF and stationed at Andrews Air Force Base when LBJ arrived in Washington, DC on that fateful day in November. I witnessed firsthand the landing of Air Force One and the extraordinary police and heavily armed FBI and Secret Service presence at the modest terminal building on base.

LBJ, as he was usually referred to, is responsible for the dramatic escalation of the Vietnam Conflict based on what has been challenged as a ruse, an incident in the Gulf of Tonkin, which led to a resolution of the same name. This resolution gave him broad powers to act without receiving prior Congressional approval. It was that vast escalation and the related military draft that aroused many of the protests of 1968.

CHAPTER 5

Evolution of a Revolution

*F*ast forward to 2020, and the United States experienced the most widespread public protests that turned violent since the 1960s.

My argument is that the underlying problem with education is the protestors and anti-war advocates of the Vietnam era went on to become the core cadre, faculty, and administrators of public schools and universities, and are now political decision makers. The 2020 antiestablishment culture is an outgrowth of an anti-war protest movement that grew to national awareness with the riots at the Democratic National Convention in Chicago in 1968.

The Civil Rights Movement

A short historical recap is useful here. Throughout the 1960s, there were a series of civil unrest incidents often immediately following some police confrontation or assassination of a popular political figure, most notably the assassination of the Reverend

Dr. Martin Luther King, Jr., (MLK) in Memphis, Tennessee. This triggered destructive riots in Washington, DC, and ten other major cities in the United States.

One of the most prominent leftist groups involved in protests in the late sixties were the Students for a Democratic Society (SDS). This was a national student activist organization in the United States during the 1960s and was one of the principal representations of the New Left. Disdaining permanent leaders, hierarchical relationships, and parliamentary procedure, the founders conceived of the organization as a broad exercise in "participatory democracy." From its launch in 1960, it grew rapidly in the tumultuous decade with over 300 campus chapters and 30,000 supporters recorded nationwide by its last national convention in 1969. The organization splintered at that convention amidst rivalry between factions seeking to impose national leadership and direction, and disputing "revolutionary" positions on, among other issues, the Vietnam War and Black Power.

A new national network for organizing left-wing students, also calling itself Students for a Democratic Society, was founded in 2006.

The core principles and arguments of the SDS are the same as much of what the 2020 protestors claim to want: The overthrow of the political establishment and an end to perceived police brutality, particularly aimed at minorities.

If you compare the photos of the turmoil of the anti-war protests in the late 1960s over the political decisions related to the Vietnam War, and the 2020 violent protests over the death of an unarmed individual in the process of being arrested you will see dramatic similarities in the appearance of the protesters and the dame that resulted from the violent acts. Many would argue that the protests over civil rights and the Vietnam war were warranted. Decades later we are still discovering that many of the statistics related to the war were incomplete and often misleading. The subsequent anti-police protests of 2020 are clearly based on incomplete and inaccurate presentation of the facts compiled by multiple authorities on the incidents of excessive use of force by police. The resulting damage is indistinguishable from the 1960s violence.

Analyses By Higher Education 'Insiders'

In his book, *The Breakdown of Higher Education: How It Happened, The Damage It Does, and What Can Be Done*, Professor John Ellis exposed the decline in the knowledge of students in higher education[20] based on his almost fifty years as a faculty member in the vaulted University of California system. In his exposé, he explains that the SDS, when they were a mere few hundred individuals espousing a Marxist agenda, held a convention in Port Huron, Michigan, and published a manifesto of that name. In it, they described how they would change the world to match their desired framework. How then were they to acquire the power that they wanted? The answer was given in the last section of their statement, "The University and Social Change," which Ellis quotes as follows:

"They would attain political power by taking over the universities: 'An alliance of students and faculty...must wrest control of the educational process from the administrative bureaucracy... They must import major public issues into the curriculum—research and teaching on problems of war and peace is an outstanding example....They must consciously build a base for their assault upon the loci of power.' Why did they choose the universities as their path to political power? Because

'The university is located in a permanent position of social influence. Its educational function makes it indispensable and automatically makes it a crucial institution in the formation of social attitudes."

Professor Ellis goes into a description of what he describes as a fantasy world on the California System university campuses and lists a catalog of courses that substitute "education" for grievance promotion. He goes on to include his analysis of how the universities' faculty changed so dramatically due to a series of three events:

"The first of these historical contingencies was the national unrest over the mishandling of the war in Vietnam by the political class. The second was the sudden massive expansion of the universities at exactly the right, or rather, the wrong time—1965 to 1975. The third was the morphing of the civil rights movement into a powerful regime of identity politics marching under the banner of 'diversity.'"

According to Ellis, the immediate culprits of this transformation were changes sparked by the "baby boom" and the Vietnam War. Dr. Ellis points out that from a demographic perspective, "In 1965 there were 3.97 million college students at American public institutions, but by 1975 that figure had more than doubled, to 8.83 million." Thus, the average public college needed to double its faculty. The colleges found their new faculty members among the recently graduated PhDs. The urgent need to fill faculty positions led to a decline in the academic standards for professors.

At the same time, Ellis explains, "The political turmoil and the unusual degree of radicalization on campus brought about by an increasingly unpopular war [in Vietnam] naturally had its greatest effect on those of draft age, which was precisely the group from which the huge expansion in college faculty numbers would have to come.

The radical faculty members made no pretense of objectivity. As older colleagues died, they gained power over committees, hiring new faculty members in their image. The campus grew less tolerant of any non-leftist viewpoint. Asking questions that critically examined extreme positions became unacceptable."

Ellis' perception of the decline in education leads me back to my original title, *Blame it on 'Nam,* and as you will see in the closing sections, the issue of not asking questions confirms that the lack of providing students with any training in critical thinking was intentional. Critical thinking would circumvent the stated goal of the Marxists who were intent on taking over education.

The Baby Boomers

The Boomers raised their offspring in the era of the 1970s and 1980s, sometimes struggling while both parents were working, as women continued to define their independence. They often left their children to be raised by preschool programs if they were economically able to do so, or left to the care of relatives. Their children, who attained maturity or coming of legal age of eighteen in 1984, is the group which the sociologists named Gen Xers. People who matured in the mid-1980s are now middle aged and in positions of influence and power as high school administrators and senior university faculty members and deans.

Generation X

Generation Xers were born between 1961 and 1981, they
matured in the 1980s and 90s and were taught by the generation
that preceded them. Strauss and Howe describe their behavior and personalities as the result of being children who were
denounced as wild and stupid. As young adults, they maneuvered
through the AIDS crisis and cautious courtship and marriage.
Politically, the group leaned pragmatic and non-affiliated and
would rather volunteer than vote. In midlife, they have battled
economic hardship and ascended into political and corporate
leadership roles, feeling like resilient survivors.

Millennials

Gen Xers are the parents of the Millennials, born 1982 to
2004, who are many of the individuals encouraging and leading
the protests in the streets of 2020. They are characteristically
described by Strauss and Howe's Life Course program as arriv-
ing among the "baby on board" signs on cars, signaling their
special status. Parenting styles shifted to teaching virtues and
values. Millennials reached their teens in the late 1990s when
volunteering and community service surged. Older skeptics argue
that Millennials were raised to think that they were special and
that getting a trophy for showing up and participating instead
of being judged for the quality and utility of their performance
has led to a lack of comprehension of the real competitive reality of life.

They began joining the workforce in the early 2000s with
employers who implemented feedback and mentorship and

career advancement programs designed to retain and promote the "best and the brightest." University and graduate students in 2020 would have been born between 1995 and 2000. If the psychologists' analyses about childhood memories are accurate, their first recall of their life experience did not register until around 2001 and the events of 9/11. They have grown up in an age of constant reminder of the risks of terrorism and the attendant wars without conclusion. Is it any wonder they are skeptical of the political leadership?

There are at least two distinct parts of this generation. Many still live at home, living life vicariously through social media on computers in their parent's basement and building acquaintances—not friends—through handheld devices. It is not considered unusual to see a group seated at the same table in a restaurant "chatting;" not among themselves, but on their cellphones with others who are not present and sharing pictures of what they are eating. Another smaller portion of the Millennials are the all-volunteer military engaged in dangerous combat in places most college students could not find on a map. Some of those military veterans are now campaigning for and winning political offices.

When asked why they are protesting, many current demonstrators show a startling lack of understanding of history or historical perspective. Apparently, the Gen Xers and older Boomers have not transferred the appreciation and comprehension of the rules and rights of citizenship very effectively to their children.

Organizations Influencing And Encouraging Dissent

What is the history of the group whose signs and slogans are the most visible in the current protests, Black Live Matter? Did they just materialize recently? No.

The 1960s also saw the rise to prominence of a Marxist organization known as the Black Panthers. The Black Panther Party (BPP), originally the Black Panther Party for Self Defense, was a revolutionary socialist political organization founded by Marxist college students Bobby Seale (Chairman) and Huey Newton (Minister of Defense) in October 1966, in Oakland, California. The party had several chapters across America and was active in the United States until 1982. Members of the BPP would openly carry weapons and monitor the behavior of the police in Oakland, with an aim to expose police brutality. They called these citizens' patrols "cop-watching."

The BPP's history is controversial. Scholars have characterized the Black Panther Party as the most influential black movement organization of the late 1960s, and "the strongest link between the domestic Black Liberation Struggle and global opponents of American imperialism." In his 1994 book, *Shadow of the Panther: Huey Newton and the Price of Black Power in America*, Hugh Pearson described the BPP as more criminal than political, characterized by "defiant posturing over substance."

Other sources referenced a 1989 book by Kenneth O'Reilly, *Racial Matters: The FBI's Secret File on Black America, 1960-1972*[21] and a book by Churchill and Vander Wall, *The COINTELPRO Papers: Documents from the FBI's Secret Wars Against Dissent in the United States,*[22] published in 2002. They describe the BPP with hindsight and argue that the FBI used questionable tactics to foment discord and conflict among the competing chapters and leadership. For example, in 1969, FBI Director J. Edgar Hoover is quoted as describing the party as "the greatest threat to the internal security of the country." He developed and supervised an extensive counterintelligence program of surveillance, infiltration, perjury, police harassment, and many other tactics, designed to undermine Panther leadership, incriminate and assassinate party members, discredit and criminalize the Party, and drain organizational resources and manpower. The FBI program is alleged to have been responsible for the assassination of Fred Hampton, and is accused of assassinating other Black Panther members, including Mark Clark, in a raid conducted by the Chicago Police.[23]

The Black Panther symbol of a raised fist in defiance was seared into the public conscience at the 1968 Olympic Games in Mexico City, when John Carlos and Tommie Smith stood on the podium with their fists raised as a "Black Power" symbol on international display after winning medals. The symbol has origins as far back as 1917 of oppressed industrial workers. It was once again seen at the conclusion of a controversial not guilty verdict in the O.J. Simpson murder trial by a juror, a former Black Panther, as O.J. left the courtroom a free man.

The current rendition of that long defunct entity is called Black Lives Matter. It is a direct manifestation of the politically misinterpreted confrontation in Ferguson, Missouri, between a young black thief and a young police officer who had been attacked in his cruiser by the victim, who was trying to wrestle the policeman's weapon from him. Michael Brown was unarmed when he was killed by the policeman after Brown turned and charged at the officer. Conflicting witness accounts, some of which were later determined to be fabrications, resulted in the policeman being exonerated of any charges. But the made-up claim and refrain of "Hands Up, Don't Shoot," from Brown's partner in crime, remains a battle cry of the BLM group and their enthusiastic supporters.

How could it be that almost no one challenges these events that are claimed to be facts, but are only based on partial evidence, biased models, incomplete data, and an image of a tiny slice in time? Why did no one ask what happened in the five minutes prior to Mr. Brown being shot or Mr. Floyd being pressed facedown on the street?

The failure to apply any semblance of critical thinking is evidence that something needs to be taught to improve our curriculum in schools. That missing skill set is the starting point of comprehending the series of events and should be the basis for subsequent action and reaction.

Summary Of Influences

We have documented evidence of a decline in the knowledge of math and English language skills levels of graduates, an understanding of the role and responsibilities of citizens and their political leaders, and little evidence of the teaching and application of critical thinking in many arenas.

We have identified some potential causes of the decline of education over nearly four decades, including a big increase in federal regulations and negotiated state and local contracts with faculty. The surge in university enrollment in the late '60s and early '70s demanded a doubling of university faculty, and the hiring and replacement of aging senior faculty was affected by political policy more than academic capabilities.

We have seen the evolution of radical '60s organizations into new renditions with the same radical objectives under a new banner. We have considered the attitudes and experiences of the normal cycle of generational change on their expectations and performance. Those generational influences have affected not only the students and how they interpret the world around them, but also the faculty, and together those interpretations affect the outcomes.

We need to consider how to use that understanding to assess possible options to improve the outcomes. The next step is how to organize and create a powerful group of similarly interested advocates who will generate an enthusiastic positive crusade to improve education and the subsequent social discourse.

CHAPTER 6

Analysis of Possible Solutions

The second phase of a reliable problem-solving mechanism is to search for possible actions that could have either prevented the problem in the first place or correct the problem once it surfaces. One key aspect is to search for successful solutions that have been implemented and either resolved or prevented similar problems by others in the past.

Summary Of The Problems

In the previous chapter we identified several problems that have adversely affected the educational outcomes of the student cohorts:

- The decline in math and reading comprehension skills evidenced by the decline in SAT scores of high school students and the general lack of understanding of American history and the rights and obligations of citizens.

- Little evidence of systematic teaching of critical thinking skills at any level in K–12 or college.
- The expansion of federal legislation and the related administrative costs at both the secondary and college level education institutions.
- The hiring and replacement of aging senior faculty caused by a surge in enrollment in the late-1960s and early-1970s that demanded doubling the faculty of universities which was affected by political policy more than academic capabilities.
- Evolution of 1960s radical groups to 2020 renditions with the same anti-establishment and societal goals and similar names and the resulting current rash of protests that often turn violent.
- The cyclical changes in generational expectations and actions that affect both students and the faculty.

Problem-Solving Opportunities

Problem solving requires us to do several things. Once we analyze the likely causes, we may be able to recommend possible solutions that could be implemented. To implement significant change, two key aspects are necessary. The individuals or groups affected by the change have to be convinced of the need to change and there must be a substantial effort to overcome or mediate the natural resistance to change. We must create an environment that is conducive to significant change.

Successful implementation also needs some enthusiastic high-level management to do the cheerleading and to oversee the implementation. Successful change management includes monitoring the progress to be sure that the desired results are being realized, and verifying that we have not just modified the problem or let it morph into something else.

Let us look at the probability of having a positive impact on each of the problems we have identified and whether an effort to make substantive change may be warranted.

1. The decline in math and reading comprehension scores and the general lack of understanding the roles and responsibilities of citizens. There are several viable alternative ways to incorporate civics teaching and improve the scores in reading and math. We can select among those proven techniques and processes that have been successful at the secondary level.

2. Little evidence of any systematic teaching critical thinking skills at either the secondary or college level. There are several programs that accomplish the goal of getting individuals to use logic and think more critically. The application of that skill is central to solving several of the other related issues.

3. The expansion of state and federal legislation and negotiated contracts. There is not much that can be effectively done in the short term to get any Congressional legislation approved that would reduce the vast volume of regulations and to reduce the costs of monitoring.

4. The hiring practices of secondary and college faculty. This is an arena that can be improved both in the short term and long term and is worthy of serious effort. Human resource management tools and techniques and reward mechanisms are readily available. There is only limited short-term potential to improve the negotiated contracts between school administrations and the faculty in the half dozen largest school districts. There is, however, potential in small and medium-sized communities to renegotiate faculty agreements, and there are thousands of those communities. Successful changes at the local level can be drivers of later change in the larger districts.

5. The current rash of protests that often turn violent. This has the most dramatic potential, but the effort is dependent on improved dialogue among the disaffected individuals who feel disenfranchised. And that intersects with developing individuals' knowledge of history, the roles and responsibilities of citizenship, and the application of critical thinking tools.

6. Generational changes between and among different age groups. Understanding of the goals and sensitivities of each generational group is central to addressing key aspects of implementing change and convincing the affected individuals and groups that there is both a need to change and a positive outcome to them from modifying their behavior.

Focus On The Solvable Problems

Let us do the easy work first. Set aside the most difficult tasks and focus our efforts on issues where we can expect to have positive short-term impact and improve the outcomes in measurable ways. Modest first steps that demonstrate positive results will empower the change agents and bring more people to the process if they see benefits arising from the early efforts.

I think it is futile to expend any serious energy in trying to get Congress to even consider educational reform. The well-funded, politically connected teachers' unions have proven in the current health crisis to wield enormous influence with the state and national legislators. There is ample evidence that classroom environments are relatively safe from becoming COVID-19 hotspots with simple protocols, but the middle aged and older faculty claim to be terrified of the virus and refuse to return to work. Unless there is a movement akin to the labor strikes in the Reagan era, in which President Reagan fired over 11,000 striking air traffic controllers, there is not much potential in the large school districts to get children back into the public learning facilities where peer interaction and one-on-one teacher/student efforts bear the most fruit.

Some arenas for positive impact exist.

There is good potential in small and midsized communities, however, to negotiate and modify existing agreements where the faculty are neighbors and friends of the parents, easy to talk to, and explain the potential benefits to both the faculty and the students of returning to a more normal environment where teachers are respected and protocols are enforced.

Many private and parochial schools have been holding classes in their facilities with very few health issues of any consequence. Children in Europe have been attending normal school classes and there are reports that they are neither susceptible to nor carriers of the dreaded Wuhan virus. Some charter schools have been conducting classes where they are not constrained by restricted use of sharing public school buildings.

The teaching techniques and discipline requirements of charter schools and parochial schools provide part of the model for improving educational outcomes. Unruly students who disrupt and harass their classmates who are honestly trying to learn need to be controlled, not coddled.

Bad behavior must have consequences or there is no incentive to behave better. Students need to learn self-respect and to be respectful of others. That skill is learned in part at home, part in an educational environment, in social and sports team interactions, and frequently in a place of worship. Part of the understanding of the rights and obligations of good citizenship includes recognizing that self-discipline and respect of others is a core responsibility of each of us.

Evidence Of The Value Of Studying Civics

The civics aspect of the education problem solving has several parts that have potential for positive outcomes and expectations of compromise.

Some examples of courses of study that have been deleted or watered down and others that have been put in place is a good starting point. A course that is still taught in some states but not in any consistent manner is civics. *Webster's* defines civics as "the social science dealing with the rights and duties of citizens."

Sarah Shapiro and Catherine Brown published an analysis of the teaching of the subject known as "civics" in the *American Educator,* Summer 2018 issue. Civics was defined as the understanding of the structure of government, and the rights and responsibilities of the citizens, including different methods of public engagement. They argued that when taught effectively, students become better informed and engaged, pointing out that the topic was not synonymous with history, but provides the students with the ability to apply what history and community service teaches. The article summarized a study, "The State of Civics Education," that the authors conducted for the Center for American Progress, where both are employed. Shapiro is a research assistant and Brown is the vice president for education policy.

They believe that the emphasis on improved reading and math scores in the K–12 curriculum has pushed the teaching of civics aside. Among the five key findings they presented is the critical lack of widespread requirements for teaching the subject, and the emphasis on knowledge rather than the application of skills and agency for civic engagement. Only two jurisdictions require community service—Maryland and the District of Columbia—although nearly half the states allow credit for community service.

They disclosed that only fourteen states require the teaching of civics and the passing of an exam on the subject to entitle students to graduate high school. Twenty-six states require a civics course. Only three states require students take a civics exam. They praised two intermountain states, Colorado and Idaho, which have innovative programs and have designed a detailed civics curriculum taught in a year-long course. They conclude that the low rates of Millennial voter participation and engagement in volunteerism indicate that schools have an opportunity to better prepare the students to fulfill the responsibilities and privileges of citizenship.

The Woodrow Wilson National Fellowship Foundation published the results of a study, part of their American History Initiative, in February 2019 of 41,000 adults who were given a multiple-choice version of the test of basic knowledge about America normally given to immigrants seeking US citizenship. Only one state, Vermont, had a barely passing grade. Sixty percent of US citizens surveyed across America overall failed the test. A quarter of those surveyed did not know that freedom of speech was a protected right under the First Amendment and only 27 percent of those under the age of forty-five had a basic understanding of US history.[24]

Clearly, the last two decades of education has not imparted a comprehensive understanding of the founding and functioning of the country in which these people are privileged to live. An essay by Meyerson and Kissel, featured in the book, *How to Educate an American*,[25] argues that there are three interacting reasons for the decline. Among them, after the collapse of the Soviet Union, there was less focus on the special value of the US Constitution; schools and colleges have prioritized other disciplines over civics; and they argue that in recent decades civic education has shifted to engagement over developing an understanding and knowledge of the Constitution.

Prevention Programs

Another study reinforces the need for more effort in K–12 of the rights and responsibilities of citizens is provided by The National Institute of Justice research brief published in July 1998 entitled "Preventing crime: What Works, What Doesn't, What's Promising."[26] In 1996, a federal law required the US attorney general to provide an independent review of the effectiveness of state and local crime prevention assistance programs that were aimed at reductions in delinquency, juvenile crime, youth gang activity, youth substance abuse, and other high-risk factors. The Department of Justice (DOJ) engaged a team of researchers from the University of Maryland to review more than 500 prevention programs and evaluate them using a standard to rank the published results on overall validity on seven dimensions.

The study identified several items for schools to incorporate and emphasize:

- Organizational development for innovation
- Communication and reinforcement of clear, consistent norms
- Teaching social competency skills
- Coaching of high-risk youth in "thinking skills"

The life skills were described as stress management, problem solving, self-control, and emotional intelligence. Those aspects are what is part of "civic citizenship" skills that includes understanding precedents and consequences.

A subject perhaps for another debate would be to compare the "citizenship" behavior of places where the subject is more thoroughly presented in K–12 with areas where it is not so well presented. That is tangential to our focus here, but the DOJ study reinforces the need to develop both a better understanding of citizens' rights and responsibilities and the application of critical thinking skills, especially in high-risk youth.

This provides us with evidence that one component of what is missing and should be included in the action plan: Increase the teaching of civics and problem solving in K–12 education.

Would there be as many protestors in the streets in 2020 if they had a better knowledge of the rights of citizenship and the consequences of violating those responsibilities? What if protestors had better critical thinking skills and could disseminate fact from propaganda?

The Common Characteristics Of Protests

Is it the location or the composition of the protestors that is more relevant? There is no safe way for private individuals to enforce curfews or civil behavior that would curb large protests. The laissez-faire attitudes of the public officials in the dozen large cities where the protests have been the most violent show no taste for punishing the violators.

Let us eliminate the easy ones first.

Location as a Factor

Location leads us to look at where is there turmoil, chaos, and disaffected individuals who are protesting? What is shown on television news and written extensively in print and posted on social media would indicate that major cities are the locale of most of the discontent. But is it the city itself that is at the center of the problem or the presence of some other activity in and around the city that amplifies the chaos?

The major antiwar protests of the late '60s were in Los Angeles, Boston, New York City, and Chicago. These are cities that are home to major universities; places where thousands of young people lived and studied. The earliest counterculture free speech protests of this era occurred on the UC Berkeley campus in the suburbs of San Francisco. Civil rights protests, on the other hand, led by the most respected civil rights leader, Martin Luther King, Jr., occurred in mid-sized Southern cities where black people were consistently mistreated and denied their civil liberties. The Reverend King's trademark was non-violent protest. What violence did occur was usually to result of overly aggressive police action and stubborn civil leadership that refused to listen to reasonable demands for civil discourse and change. The marchers themselves were peaceful—then.

MLK's assassination in Memphis sparked riots in cities across America, most notably Louisville, Baltimore, and Washington, DC. Surprisingly, his hometown of Atlanta was spared large-scale protests over his death. Atlanta is the home of four historically black colleges and yet, there were few protests over MLK's assassination at the time. Not so with the more recent altercation over the shooting of a black man after he passed out in his car, blocking the drive-thru lane of a fast-food restaurant. When the Atlanta police explained they had to arrest him, he suddenly wrestled free from them and stole the taser from one of the policemen.

He was fleeing the police when he turned and appeared to shoot at the cops who were pursuing him. That case has yet to be adjudicated and I suspect that an Atlanta jury will find the officer overreacted to the threat. In the immediate aftermath, an entire building was destroyed and, along with it, the livelihood of the franchisee and his entire staff. I know a bit about the fast-food franchise business and there were probably fifty or more employees who almost always are nearby residents working part time. They are all now out of work.

The recent BLM protests have occurred in mid-sized cities and larger ones. Some were related to the site of an event that triggered the protests, while others materialized in hours after calls to action on social media in locations not directly involved in the activity being protested.

Cities may be the locale of many large-scale protests, but it also indicates that the presence of large numbers of young people who are not fully employed or in school and otherwise occupied that provides the bulk of the protestors.

This leads me to the conclusion that it is safe to discount location as a factor and move to more fertile characteristics and to focus on the participants. Perhaps better employment opportunities for recent graduates would help, but that also requires that the graduates study topics for which there is a need and a market.

Composition of Protestors

Are there any common attributes to students who have been taught an accurate history of the American experience, especially the advances made by minorities over the past three decades, who demonstrate objectively that they know how to read critically and apply mathematical problem solving to everyday activities versus the academic studies of many of the protestors? What subjects are being taught in their educational institutions that are different than the topics presented in institutions located in communities in turmoil? We have already talked about the importance of teaching civics to students at the K–12 level.

What about the university level? That is where most of the protestors come from. What is it in the university environment that promotes the idea that violent street protests are an appropriate way to express yourself?

Professor Ellis is clear and forceful in his conclusion. He argues that radicals have taken over academia and the only solution is to remove them from positions of influence. He points out that individuals, families, and government are spending huge sums of money to pay for a product—a college degree—that is defective. He reminds his readers that this is not a cyclical change that will right itself and return to the long-established traditions of an academia where ideas are presented and students and faculty are encouraged to engage in spirited, civil debates. His conclusion, substantiated with numerous examples and citations from other authors, is that radical left activists, unable to establish their agenda through the ballot box, instead took over higher education and with it came the dismantling of traditional education.

The core of his argument is "the general aim of reform must always be that those campus units and structures in which excellence in teaching and research has been replaced by fervent radical activism and identity politics must be dismantled, defunded, removed." He presents several ideas that include community-level action with local school boards, challenging the rules and roles of state-sponsored entities charged with the responsibility for oversight of higher public education. That is one approach to solving the problem, but the takeover of academia didn't occur abruptly. It occurred incrementally over three decades and there are legal impediments to simply firing the offensive faculty and removing the courses they have infiltrated and the agenda of "diversity" and "victimization" they replaced them with.

However, Ellis does provide some encouragement. Not all university areas have been compromised and corrupted, namely, the STEM field, and some small part of the humanities and social sciences. He argues they remain at risk if no positive action is taken to reduce or remove the political activists from the classrooms and boardrooms. There still exists on campus, often in the engineering and business schools, a remnant of the more traditional role of education. What is it that engineers and businesspeople learn that provides the skills to succeed?

For engineers, there is a heavy emphasis on math and physical sciences—topics that are not subject to good or bad debate. The rules simply exist. The universe functions in a reliably structured way that can be predicted and, to some extent, managed by controlling the inputs and the application of known elements. Business schools focus on management, organization skills, accountability, and rewards based on performance. Topics that are essential to evaluating and selecting productive courses of action, both on an organizational as well as personal level. As a professor of management accounting at three different US universities, I know of only two individuals out of the thousand or so students I interacted with who were journalism majors attending a business school class.

We need to incorporate the skills needed to develop and appreciate those core attributes into the K–12 curriculum. Ellis admits that reform measures will have to begin on a small scale, in a few states where political opinion is hospitable. Those two aspects are central to the proposed action plan to follow.

Charter Schools

Another means of changing the education at the K–12 level are charter schools. This concept is an outgrowth according to Thomas Sowell, noted scholar at Stanford, from the controversies following the US Supreme Court decision in Brown v. Board of Education. Sowell argues that decision led to a crusade to provide alternatives that would improve the options for black, inner city students. Bussing was tried and generally failed and was deeply unpopular in both white and black communities.

Homeschooling is an option that can work, but it requires a stay-at-home parent who has the knowledge, the skills, and the patience to teach their offspring what should be presented in public schools. Parochial schools benefited to some degree from the decision as well and survive as a viable alternative, but carry with it a religious training that some parents are uncomfortable with for a variety of reasons. Charter schools enjoy a combination of state and community support in physical facilities, yet are less constrained in the curriculum and teaching approaches they use to engage the students.

There are more successful charter schools than unsuccessful ones; victims of market constraints. If the charter schools do not produce positive results, then enrollment falters and the programs are discontinued. But, there are some powerful entities that are hostile to the idea of charter school programs, and that is the focus of Sowell's 2020 book, *Charter Schools and Their Enemies*. Although charter schools are a small segment of the education sector—according to Sowell, less than 10 percent of the students in K–12 nationwide—there are those who are hostile. They include teachers' unions, schools of education, and some politicians who control the millions in public education funding. Sowell claims there are over 50,000 students on waiting lists for charter schools in New York City alone; a city where the per-pupil expenditure in over $20,000 a year in government funding. And that billion dollars a year is what is at the heart of much of the resistance to expanding the charter school programs. At the root of the resistance is money and the shifting of resources from areas controlled by politically connected unions and their heavily sponsored political allies.

Those hostile to the changes in K–12 education are some of the same voices that will have to be convinced to overcome the natural resistance to change that we will be discussing later in our plan of action. While the pro/con rationale and arguments of charter schools are of interest and are worthy of investigation and resolution, they are not directly germane to the issue of this book, and that is what needs to be taught as opposed to where the teaching occurs. I encourage my readers who have young students and are looking at alternative school options, but may have only seen press reports of the success vs. failure of charter schools, to read Sowell's enlightening book. But be patient, the waiting lines for admission are long for the good charter schools.

Improving Education

The Thomas B. Fordham Institute published a collection of essays titled, *How to Educate an American,* edited by Michael J. Petrilli and Chester E. Finn, Jr.[27] The two editors are the president and president emeritus of the Thomas B. Fordham Institute. The book looks at education in four parts: History, Civics, and Citizenship; Character, Purpose, and Striving; Schools, Family, and Society; and Renewing a Conservative Education Agenda. Petrilli and Finn's conclusion summarizes the contributions of a dozen respected individuals including The Honorable Lamar Alexander, former senator from Tennessee who was influential in passing the ESSA law in the Obama administration, and The Honorable William J. Bennett, former US secretary of education in the Reagan administration, along with professors from

86

Harvard's Kennedy School of Government, Johns Hopkins University School of Advanced International Studies, Stanford University, Princeton, and the American Enterprise Institute, among other authors of national reputation. Some of the contributions are cited elsewhere in this book.

Petrilli and Finn close the summary with the optimistic perspective that agreement and compromise remain possible, even on Capitol Hill. But they acknowledge that effective change in primary and secondary education will be chiefly accomplished at the state, district, and local school boards.

Parents and the teachers at individual schools must become the core advocates for change. That is who this book is directed to and included in our plan of action is a set of relatively easy-to-implement activities to encourage and develop community support for effective change.

Leadership Skills Development

What about leadership and community involvement? Is there any evidence that those attributes, when developed on a broad scale, lead to calmer, less confrontational debate?

Several organizations, primarily aimed at young men, had been influential in the development of codes of conduct and promoting individual self-reliance and advancing the knowledge of civic involvement. Two standouts that have been active for at least three generations are the Scouts and Jaycees.

The Scouts organization was founded in 1910 on the principles of teaching boys about patriotism, courage, and self-reliance. It was one of a dozen organizations to receive a federal charter. Originally called the Boy Scouts, its peak membership in

1973 was 4 million members. The organization has struggled in recent years, mainly as the result of social changes and a US Supreme Court decision mandating changes in the membership requirements to not discriminate based on both the gender and sexual identity of members and adult leaders. Membership is now estimated at less than 2.3 million. In a country of 330 million residents, that represents less than one percent of the population.

Founded in 1920, the United States Junior Chamber of Commerce, better known as the Jaycees, was organized to provide young men opportunities to develop personal and leadership skills through service to others, individual training, acquiring management skills, and understanding business development. They boast that the organization has helped 12 million young adults in the US and 20 million worldwide to become leaders in their communities. Its membership peaked in 1976 at about 356,000 men between the ages of 18 and 35. After a Supreme Court antidiscrimination ruling in 1984, the organization now includes women. Current membership is about 12,000 in 400 communities.

Clearly, neither entity is any longer a significant influence maker. The decline in both organizations parallels the "coming of age" of the Gen Xers, and it is their offspring, the Millennials, that are the majority of the people protesting in the streets now. These two societal changes are further evidence of the influence of the anti-war protestors as explained by Professor Ellis and others, and referenced in my book titles original title.

Combatting Liberal Bias

How can the community at large overcome the influence of the liberal bias that has been taught in the colleges and universities and has since been pulled down into the classrooms in high schools? What is missing in the education process that might improve the decision-making process on social policy and generate vigorous debate, not violent street protests?

The question becomes how to encourage eighteen to twenty-five-year-olds to become more civic minded, more inclined toward calm polite discourse to address social issues, and more discerning in what sources of information they rely on and what "truth" they believe. Revising or reeducating them will be more difficult than to train and inform young minds in the first place. But that doesn't mean we should abandon them and simply write off those protestors as another "lost generation." Our action plan suggests a relatively easy program that can be introduced at minimal cost that will mediate this.

Advocates need to pick the fights they can win. Evaluating possible solutions includes eliminating or not wasting effort on emotional issues that will prove distracting and result in an unproductive use of time and resources. Don't dilute your efforts on emotional issues. This is more likely to just add to the frustration and delay the time to implement meaningful changes.

Elimination of counterproductive material that is not factually correct could be another goal of our advocates. Eliminating an entire subject is not necessary and we can avoid the resistance by taking a different tactical approach. The emotional disagreement over the founding of the country is an element that does not need to be front and center. But it is likely to be a counterargument, so advocates need to be prepared to keep the improvement in the curriculum focused on what will benefit the students.

The 1619 Project Example

Instead of arguing for the removal of a subject, such as the *New York Times'* controversial 1619 Project, we should be advocating for the inclusion of programs to improve critical thinking skills. If the reader or listener to the arguments of the 1619 Project has developed the skills of being a critical thinker, challenges the authors' credentials and experience, and understands any potential bias and/or profit motive in presenting a historically inaccurate viewpoint, then the 1619 Project's argument may fail to be convincing.

To accomplish that, advocates need to know more about what is in the inaccurate material and be prepared to provide a counterargument based on fact. In Chapter 4 we briefly introduced this flawed material. Advocates of change need to be fully armed with a knowledge of the content and objectives of this material to be able to deflect and focus on what will overcome the bias, even if it is presented to the students. Here is a brief summary of the problem and its source. This is a good example of how to learn about a controversial program and create your argument.

An article was printed in the *New York Times Magazine* in August 2019 promoting a redefinition of the effect of slavery which argued that the establishment and growth of the United States was built on the backs of black slaves and that the country is based on racist policy because some of the founders were slave owners. It is a controversial perspective that has aroused passions on both sides of the issue. For many people, this is troubling because the program has been adopted by some school districts and includes courses taught to children as young as the first and second grades.

Balanced History

Part of the problem is the actual life work of many of the founders of America is ignored or discounted. Yes, many of the men were owners of agricultural businesses and in those times, much of the labor was provided by indentured servants and slaves. Students rarely get a comprehensive picture of the era due to the reduction or outright elimination of American history, coupled with the short-term memory of the twenty-first century. Student and teacher populations often fail to present events in the context of history and ignore even the formal published writings of the founders that argued that separation was a first step to recognizing that all individuals are created equal. Many historians believe that the founders intended that statement as formally acknowledging the obligation to end the practice of slave labor in the new republic.

Also dismissed or ignored are the efforts over the past three hundred years to correct those early abuses. Even within the black academic community, there is bitter disagreement between those who see the growth and liberty and success of black people versus those who focus on the inner city communities and argue that they are still disadvantaged solely because of their skin color. Most rational observers argue that the failure of the poor and unemployed black or white individual is most often due to a combination of poor parenting decisions and a lack of education in skills that enable worthwhile and well-compensated employment opportunities.

A central issue to the problem of the education of those inner city communities is that the public schools that are available are failing miserably in even teaching the basics. What is needed is school choice, as pointed out earlier with Sowell's evaluation of the resistance to charter schools. But that is a political argument and one that has entrenched resistance because of the vast sums of money under the control of politicians and influence of well-funded unions.

Civics, some history, and learning the rights and responsibilities of citizens, if understood by the students in K–12, would provide an alternative explanation for the circumstances faced by many, especially in the inner city minority communities. Advocates for change need to focus on the benefits of teaching and building life skills with civics and critical thinking, not get sidetracked in emotional arguments about who, how, or why the founders wanted to create a "more perfect union."

CHAPTER 7

Action Plan

*I*f you have read this far, then you have the facts and the knowledge you need and are ready to move into an Action Plan phase to implement the changes needed to improve the ability of students to think critically and to understand why those life skills are valuable. If we are fortunate to also get your public school to increase the focus on the rights, privileges, and responsibilities of citizens, too, then we could have a double win.

You are about to get a return on your investment in time and all for the modest cost of this book. What it is worth to you is personal. What follows is my gift to you for being persistent and motivated to bring an effective change to your local school that will positively impact your children and your community. I will share the tools and techniques I have taught to scores of young university students, some of whom went on to win competitions in debates.

I will share the key elements of skills I have learned as a young military trainer, later as a university lecturer and an assistant professor, and as an occasional professional actor. I have been fortunate to have had the benefit of some talented mentors and I am happy to share their counsel with you.

I will share the process of managing change. There are proven procedures and activities developed to accomplish the goal of successfully implementing any significant change. My PhD dissertation dealt with how to implement information system change in organizations, and I had a consulting assignment with a large company that had just been relieved of public utility regulations and restrictions and had gone on a buying frenzy of smaller, private entities. I have some firsthand experience in managing change.

I will show you proven communication techniques to improve your chances to have your message listened to, understood, and acted upon, instead of just being heard. I will also share some suggestions for understanding where the listener is coming from to improve your success in having your message not only understood, but that you get an appropriate feedback response and a commitment to act. Those skills will help you to deal with your family, the neighbors, elected school board officials, and school managers and teachers. It may even improve conversations within your workplace and among your close friends and associates.

Managing Change

The first hurdle in implementing a change is to convince the affected people of a need to change their mind or their behavior. That means starting with convincing them of the need to change and describing the benefits they will obtain in doing so. In the implementation phase you need to encourage the participants as they work through the stages and to monitor their progress in measurable steps. It doesn't end when the change has been made. There is a requirement to assess whether the changes implemented are having the desired effect or if the issue has merely morphed into a different problem.

On an organizational level, we need to identify the decision makers who can be influenced into making a substantive change in the curriculum. I will present summaries of the background on the generational groups that we have to consider, as there are at least three quite different worldviews held by each successive generation that affect how they see the problem and how they are going to react to a challenge to change the situation. Some people are going to be easier to reach and persuade.

It is not sufficient to merely propose a change and to argue that it will improve the outcomes of some perceived problem. Managing change requires us to provide a valid, rational reason to change, and to convince the affected individuals that a change is not only needed but that it will provide a benefit to them. We have discussed what may seem to us today to be a dramatic change in university faculty focus and K–12 classroom presentations. But that change has not happened overnight. It has been two generations in development.

In the prior chapter we asked the rhetorical question about what is missing in the process that might improve the decision-making skills that affect social policy and generate a vigorous debate without the violent protests.

There are two groups of participants that must be convinced to change their behavior to improve the educational outcomes: The teachers and professors who deliver the content and the message; and the students. But, the students are really represented by the parents—the ones who are either funding the education through local taxes or writing tuition checks.

It is the college students and recent graduates of college and university programs that are flooding the streets and protesting, encouraged by the faculty who have indoctrinated them, and tolerated by the political class who have restricted the response and reduced the penalties for bad behavior. Ellis pointed out clearly that in his university system, the faculty include self-selected, like-minded liberal thinkers who now dominate the classrooms and the management. This is true of many colleges and universities.

Our goal is to modify not only the overall goals and management of education in the mid- and long-term time frame, but in the short run to improve the decision-making skills of the students by adding just one or two courses taught in K–12 and the first year of university education: civics and critical thinking. The short term must demonstrate an effective alternative to the argumentative social discourse currently in full bloom, or the mid- and long-term goals will never materialize.

Demographics of the Key Stakeholders

Who are the players in this drama? There is a huge potential population that can be impacted by improving the educational process. The overall population distribution in the United States of America, according to projections done in late 2019 indicates there are almost 82 million people under the age of twenty, and about 45 million in their twenties. Both groups are evenly divided between males and females. The 2019 projection shows almost

83 million Gen Xers out of the entire population estimated to be 328 million. One-fourth of the population.[28]

In the prior discussion we have presented some of the issues based on the experiences of different generations. Understanding the mix of participants and where they are in their careers will be helpful in implementing successful change. The chart below based on Rudd birth year allocations indicates the expected position in a normal growth from school into the work force and probable career path up through the ranks.

Generation	Birth Years	Age in 2020	Career Path Progress
Boomers	1943 - 1960	60 to 77	At or Near Retirement
Gen Xers	1961 - 1981	39 to 59	Mid or Upper Management
Millenials	1982 - 2004	16 to 38	School or Early Career
Homelanders	2005 - on	Infants to 15	Learners

We will have success if we effectively demonstrate how the changes proposed meet the goals and expectations of each different group of participants. That means we need to look at the change from their perspective.

Anyone who is eager to improve the educational outcomes needs to evaluate the individual members of your local school board, the local political leaders, and the politically active members of the local educators. The odds are they are going to be a mix of at least two generations and possibly three.

The primary long-term beneficiaries of our efforts will be the current generation of young students, the Homelanders, and the younger members of the Millennial generation still in the classrooms of our high schools and colleges.

Without top management support, most organizational change falters. Let's look at the national level and get a sense of the top-down leadership. Then we can evaluate what influences need to be overcome to get the actual classroom environment more conducive to improving the life skills of the students. Skills that enable them to make reasoned decisions based on facts, and to be able to differentiate between the facts and propaganda or opinion.

How Different Generations Respond to Change

Our real objective is to improve the life skills learned and that will require us to look at the goals and expectations of the generation doing the teaching, not just those of the students being taught. The generation currently in K–12, the Homelanders, were born post-2005. Their early life memories as explained previously do not recall much of anything prior to age five, the year 2010. They have a distinctly different worldview than their parents or grandparents. This is the generation we have the best short-term opportunity to impact while they are still learning the basics.

To do that we have to convince the school boards who make the curriculum decisions, and the teachers who deliver the material, to modify the content and delivery in their classrooms. It will be a political battle in some communities, and not so difficult in others. The readers who choose to become reformer advocates need to pick their early battles in places where the population is amenable to change and the politicians are accommodating. Once some success is demonstrated, then the reformers will have better ammunition to combat the entrenched bureaucracy in the larger school districts.

The academic mentors and senior faculty are likely in their middle age, late-thirties to mid-fifties. Projecting from Strauss, the senior administrators and political leaders are most likely older Gen Xers, but the classroom teachers and college lecturers are most likely Millennials. They have decidedly different worldview especially on education and parenting.

Millennials were raised by Gen Xers and influenced by Boomers, who often had a laissez-faire approach to parenting. Experts in the field of generational change point out that it was the hands-off parenting of the Boomers that caused the Gen Xer reaction, which resulted in their being more involved in their child's upbringing and to actively participate in the education process. The Boomers, if they considered the issue at all, just assumed that the teachers and professors were the same dedicated folks they had in the '50s and '60s, and we now know that is not true.

The result, according to experts like Strauss[29], is that the Millennials are much more protective of their offspring and more actively involved in the parent-teacher organizations. As the Millennials entered the professional ranks and began working up the career ladder, the attitudes and core issues they brought to the workplace included the perceived prestige of the teaching profession, the civic purpose of education, and the workload aspects that provided the opportunity for a balanced life with more free time and regular holidays than many other occupations. Those perspectives and attitudes towards education should make them amenable to change.

How Can Change Benefit the Teachers?

If the advocates for reform posture the changes in a way that directly improves one of the key attributes that teachers are said to appreciate, that is, emphasizing the prestige of being a teacher. Having students who are more respectful and less problematic in their classrooms is a direct tangible benefit for the teachers. By providing the support materials and teaching guides, teachers don't have to develop the curriculum from scratch to accomplish these improvements. This should be appreciated as well, since they have selected a profession that provides ample time for personal pursuits.

Strauss predicted that Gen X parents would expect to have transparency and access to information, including the credentials of their childrens' teachers, and want the best outcomes for their offspring. Both Millennials and Gen Xers are also more technologically comfortable than Boomers and willing to entertain new approaches that result in work-life balance and are outcome focused more than process focused. That should make them good candidates for well thought out changes in the subjects taught and the ways in which they are presented that will engage their children, especially the younger Homelander generation.

That's the good news.

Roadblocks

The bad news, or at least a bigger challenge, is the fact that many of the top political leaders are elder Boomers, some of whom are long past the average retirement age, but unwilling to step aside. Some have expressed frustration with the younger generations they considered to be lazy and undisciplined kids. The top leaders in the US Congress are all elder Boomers: Pelosi is eighty, Schumer is seventy-nine, McConnell is seventy-eight, and the recently elected President Biden is seventy-eight years old. Some appear to be more interested in protecting their perceived prestige as leaders and the process than in the actual outcomes.

The current president of the national American Federation of Teachers (AFT), Randi Weingarten, is sixty-three, among the later born group of Boomers and nearing regular retirement age. She is the daughter of a teacher. Her worldview was shaped by her mother, who was involved in a seven-week strike. The then teenaged Ms. Weingarten and some of her eleventh-grade classmates conducted a survey that they presented to the school board, which modified their budget cuts and retribution of the striking teachers. A lawyer by profession, Weingarten successfully litigated high-level grievances for the United Federation of Teachers (UFT), and she also has classroom experience. She has been president of the AFT union since 2008 and the first openly gay leader of a national labor union. Her view of school reform she describes as "bottom up" and that public officials should welcome the view of teachers when helping schools better serve their students. She is a defender of tenure for teachers and a critic of charter schools.

The just appointed US Secretary of Education, Miquel Cardona, is a Gen Xer born in 1975, the middle of that generation. He is a former teacher who was appointed commissioner of education of his home state of Connecticut in 2019. As a child, he spoke only Spanish at home and has admitted to struggling upon his entry to an English language public school. His dissertation as a PhD student at UConn (2011) dealt with the political issues of non-native English speaking learners. Cardona has had a meteoric career path and reached a political peak professionally at middle age, compared to what most would consider the normal career path. His professional experience is relatively unknown to most. If he exhibits the traits of a stereotypical middle-aged Gen Xer, he is likely to be looking for stability and safe harbors for himself and should be open to addressing issues that would calm the educational environment.

What I cannot presume or predict is the composition of the local school boards in your area. What I can do is provide some guidance based on the work of experienced professionals by outlining the likely goals and aspirations of the two groups that must be convinced of the need to change the content and methods of presentation in their schools.

Earlier, we also raised the issue of the legality of using classrooms as a platform for the presentation of a particular political ideology, and to object if it is presented without any discussion of contrary opinions or facts. Citizen reformers who are eager to challenge the local board of education would do well to carefully read the current regulations and empowering legislation that authorizes and provides for the supervision of the public education in their district and state.

The Role of Parents

Parents need to become actively involved in personally reviewing the reading assignments of their children and to engage in discussion at home about what they are learning in class. Boomer parents were too busy climbing the career ladder to do that. Gen X and Millennial parents are much more likely to make the time to be active participants in understanding what their children are being taught, to be engaged in their parent-teacher associations, and to attend public meetings of the governing school boards. It is in those meetings, formal or informal, that the individuals who are eager to make changes can evaluate the leadership and determine who may become an ally in the cause, and, just as importantly, who will likely object to change. Knowledge of the perspectives and goals of each of those two groups is crucial to being effective in encouraging and overcoming resistance to change.

The Statista summary of age groups reveals there were almost 83 million US residents between the ages of 40 and 59, the Gen X population, in 2019. Given the size of the generational population and the stage of their careers, let us start with a summary of some key issues in dealing with Gen Xers. Sandra Rudd[30] published a useful summary of characteristics of four generations and among the extensive details she amassed are a few key issues that the reader can use in improving communication. By focusing our quest to just two specific courses, we stand a far better chance of success, than if we simply say something vague like "we want educational outcomes to improve."

Focus on the Benefits to Your Audience

When I was teaching a business and professional communications course, I advised my freshman students that every listener had a radio station playing in their head: WIFM. This stands for What's In it For Me. If they wanted to get their message listened to and understood, then focus on results and how they impact the individual you are talking to and make it relevant to their perspective and in a way that considers their background and experience.

Communication Styles and Generations

Rudd suggests that Gen Xers prefer direct, straight talk using their language and informal communication styles. Tethered to their cell phones, we need to keep the messages brief and stress results. Gen Xers see training as a way to enhance their own versatility in the marketplace, so explain how your recommendations will improve the versatility and ability of the young adults in their classrooms. They take a proactive approach and are not loyal to one employer, but rather loyal to themselves. Rudd believes they adapt well to change, are good multitaskers, and are not intimidated by authority. They tend to be skeptical, impatient, and technologically savvy. Gen Xers value information.

If you want to reform education by including the subject of critical thinking ask a teacher a question on some relevant current topic they are interested in. For example, "If you had known XX information, would you have made the same choices?" Listen carefully to their answer and watch for body language clues. Then explain that the concept of using critical thinking skills, like asking half a dozen key questions, would give them and their students a more complete understanding of the facts. That should lead to improved calmer communications and better results. And this is what we want our children to be taught in school so they are better informed and make good choices.

Millennials, on the other hand, are comfortable with intangibles. Rudd suggests they prefer polite, positive, motivational communication that uses action verbs and language that paints a picture. They prefer to learn in teams, be entertained in the process, and want to do meaningful work. They like it when provided with structure and get recognition for their heroes, including grandparents. Millennials are willing and eager to take risks and consider making mistakes a learning experience.

The younger cohorts of this generation are still in school and will be the direct, immediate beneficiaries of learning how to better gather information and sort through the maze of data at their fingertips. If we are successful in getting the younger members of this generation to join the movement to improve their ability to succeed, they will be immensely helpful in convincing their parents to participate and cooperate.

Communications Cycle

There is a common joke that was once even on a poster in the '70s that went something like, "I know you think you understood what I said but that isn't what I meant." The skill a good communicator practices is not mysterious. It is not something they are magically endowed with at birth, but a skill set learned and consistently applied. As a teacher, I knew that humor was a necessary element in getting my audience to pay attention, so

I bravely drew a silly picture on the board of two stick figures and proceeded to explain with arrows and notes the usual cycle of communications. I will reproduce a facsimile of that here with the benefit of computer graphics.

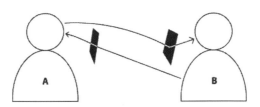

The cycle goes as follows: Person A thinks of something to say, a message to send to Person B and speaks words that Person B hears, or writes words that Person B reads. Person B receives what Person A sent, interprets what they heard, and responds with feedback to Person A. Person A receives the feedback, interprets it, and responds.

However, note the clumsy image of a barrier between both Persons A and B that interrupts the smooth flow of the message between them. Each has a filter through which they hear or read, and that filter determines what they understand of the message. How they interpret the message determines how they respond.

Everyone has a filter through which they interpret what message they receive, regardless of how it is delivered. Filters are made up of the combination of our life experiences including our age, gender, education, cultural or religious beliefs, native language, and experience. Spoken communication is a combination of both the physical aspects of sound, tone, and energy which is about 80 percent of the message, and the words themselves, which represent just 20 percent.

Think back to a time when you were young, and your mother called you. Compare your reaction to when the voice from the other room was soft and pleasant like an invitation to come have lunch, or when you left a mess someplace or failed to execute some task you had been assigned. My favorite example was a story Tony Robbins told on the topic. He said it was clearly a vastly different message when his mom called cheerfully, "Tony? Its lunch time," and the deeper voice with a harder edge saying "Anthony!" All of us would know immediately that mom was not happy.

Dealing with Filters

So how do we apply the knowledge of the existence of this filter? We can't see it, and if we do not know the other person well, we don't have a good measure of it. But we can learn about it from observation and research. Since we are discussing how to prepare for a conversation with an elected official, we have access to a lot of information that we would not normally have about an average stranger. There are election materials where the candidate proudly describes their background and all the reasons why you should vote for them. There may be public testimony or articles written in the news or an interview on local radio or television that demonstrates claims of their expertise and provides clues about their point of view.

In today's social media environment, there is more information than we need in public view of their perspectives and opinions. An easier, quicker way is to attend meetings where they are participants and listen, take notes, and ask questions. That will help you choose the most likely member of the board to be open to the request for change and to focus your presentation on them. It can also provide a guide to the most appropriate words and phrases and analogies to get the listener to hear accurately and understand what you mean.

Whichever method you chose to use, DO the research. Know who you are talking to and what hot buttons they have—some you will want to avoid and others you will want to emphasize. I insisted that my students provide at least three research references for any topic they presented, a carryover from days I was a CPA who advised contractors to get at least three bids on a project. We will talk about how to do the research later when we discuss the application of effective critical thinking skills.

The Three Ps

A simple key I encouraged my students to understand when making a persuasive argument is what I call the Three Ps: Be Prepared. Be Polite. Be Persistent.

One of the authors I referenced in class, Richard Zeoli in his book, *The 7 Principles of Public Speaking,* stated that to become an effective public speaker, make it personal and become a storyteller.[31] People care more about emotion and will remember that more than the details of a story. For example, if you know a story of a successful adult/child exchange that demonstrates the child's use of critical thinking or the knowledge of civics, use that to get the attention of the school board member or the principal of the school. Ask the teacher or the board member if they have children and if they do, are their children attending public school? If they are, then use that to reinforce what their children are not now learning to make your point. If their children are not attending public school, then ask them why not? What does the private school have that they send their children to that the public school doesn't offer?

What clues are there that we may observe to determine if we are having an effective communication? People all have habits, what gamblers call "tells," and there are both verbal and nonverbal signs of poor listening habits. Verbally the listener may interrupt, change the subject, or talk over the other person. Nonverbal examples are signs of impatience, like fidgeting or looking at their watch. A person may have their arms folded across their chest and make no eye contact. Sometimes people are pretending to listen but their mind is elsewhere.

Think about our own listening habits. Are you close-minded, opinionated, insincere, inattentive, or lazy? You need to listen carefully to the response you get and interpret that accurately. How do we know if we are accurately interpreting what we hear? Ask a question, or paraphrase what we *think* we heard and ask for confirmation. Take an inventory of your own listening skills. The book *Business and Professional Communication* [32] recommends to limit your own talking, avoid interrupting, concentrate, make positive comments, control your emotions, and listen for feelings.

Another old textbook I found made some points that were helpful in building my students' communications skills was the use of language, *Present like a Pro.*[33] Use words to paint a picture. Avoid 'weak" verbs such as hope, wish, want, and avoid buzzwords and jargon. Know the main point you want to make that adds value for the listener and repeat it a little differently at least twice more.

Get Organized and Time Conscious

The next step to making an effective presentation is to get organized. That will reduce the stress that is inherent in any public conversation and makes it possible to provide a coherent argument with smooth transitions and a clear conclusion... and in a reasonably short period of time. My mantra for short informative talks was, "Tell 'em." Tell them what you are going to tell them, tell them, then tell them what you told them.

In school board meetings, public comments may be limited to a specific amount of time. Know that constraint and build your presentation to fit it. I trained my students to a recommended budget of their time. Never make an introduction that is more than 10 percent of the time allotted and make a clear concise summary not more than 20 percent of your time. That means you should make your specific points in the remaining 70 percent. For example, if you are limited to a five-minute time frame, you can't spend more than thirty seconds on "hellos and thanks for the opportunity," and stating what you plan to talk about. (Five minutes is 300 seconds, 10 percent of that is thirty seconds). Summarize the two main points at the end and, if possible, make a call to action for the listener.

Practice Makes Perfect

The key to any presentation is practice. Most of you reading this book are not professional speakers, but with some guidance and practice, you can present like one. I recommended my students write out their presentation, read it aloud at least three times and know the content. Time it and then include a "fudge factor" of time for the stress of the actual presentation and the effect that may have on your pace. Some folks talk faster when they are nervous, others slower. Know yourself.

If your remarks can be read, then write it out in large enough type you can read from arm's length on top of a podium or lectern. Otherwise, make simple note cards of the key points that will serve as memory cues. And smile. Make eye contact with each of the target audience You will know by the physical response whether they are listening, in agreement or not, and you can use that feedback to determine if you are getting your message across.

Finally, I urged them to practice in front of a mirror. Discover if you have some distracting physical habit like a headshake or tossing your hair. One of the worst offenses is frequent "uuhs," "ummms," and "ahhs." In a longer presentation, your audience will ignore what you say while they count how many times you do that. How do we avoid that common distraction? Think with your mouth closed and learn to not let these unintended sounds escape when you are gathering your thoughts.

Do the Research

Do research into the background of the individuals to whom you are talking. You also need to know specifically what the local school board rules and regulations are concerning curriculum development. What is the current state of the courses being taught in your area schools and how effective is that process? Before we jump into research, let's take a step back and look at how to discern which sources of information are reliable. Think of it as an exercise in applying the critical thinking skills this book is encouraging you to insist the school board add to the curriculum of your schools.

Asking Questions

Previously, I summarized some of the points and processes developed by Browne and Keeley. Their book, *Asking the Right Questions,* includes eleven specific questions to use. For my students' purposes, we only needed to focus on a small subset to get them beyond the high school habit of cutting and pasting a Wikipedia article and claiming to have done "research." Wikipedia is an excellent starting point, especially if you just want a few highlights or a recap of the topic. But I urged them to go to the footnotes and read the original work cited to be sure they were getting an accurate summation of the work done by others.

My students were first semester freshman with no more than basic math skills and most of them were non-native English speakers. For them, the choice of words and the application of skeptical analysis took on a bigger challenge. I share that because I speculate that most of my readers are not trained in statistics or the evaluation of evidence and the understanding of the differences between coincidence versus cause and effect. Not to fear, you don't have to become a sophisticated research analyst. Logic will prevail if you apply it regularly and have a basic understanding of the true meaning of a few key words and phrases.

Correlation or Cause and Effect?

There is a material difference between correlation and cause and effect. Many people not trained in statistical analysis confuse coincidence with correlation. Coincidence is when events happen at the same time and appear to be related, but are not. Correlation is a more precise term applied to phenomena or variables that occur in a relationship that is consistent and not subject to mere chance. Academics are fond of using the expression "statistically significant" in their description of the results of the studies they conduct. Without getting into the weeds, that phrase means that the results are expected to occur most of the time, only at the fringes. What that means to a layperson is that the probability of the events occurring merely by chance is remote.

Here is a simple example of cause and effect that may help demonstrate the relationship. A carpenter hits a nail with a hammer and drives it into a piece of wood. The blow by the hammer is the cause, the penetration of the wood by the nail is the effect. The fact that an observer was standing next to the carpenter is merely coincidence. The carpenter did not require the presence of the observer to accomplish the task of putting the two pieces of wood together. However, if the observer is the direct supervisor of the carpenter and instructed the carpenter to combine the two pieces of wood to form a frame for a wall, then there is a correlation between the instruction and the action. But, the instruction did not cause the nail to penetrate the wood, the hammer did.

I explained to my students that with respect to information, especially "news," they needed to ask four simple "W" questions:

Who, When, Why, What. Who wrote it? When was it written? Why was it written? What inside information or expertise does the writer have that would make us accept what they presented as true? I don't think the readers of this book are likely to be naive enough to not recognize that much of the printed news and most of the television coverage is biased to one perspective or another. Naive individuals are not likely to have invested the money to buy this book or the time to read it this far.

The important keys to being a discerning consumer of information is to read carefully and decide if any of the words or phrases used are subject to more than one interpretation. Some of the points made by Browne and Keeley are to ask if there are any conflicts or assumptions made by the author or presenter? And, in particular, are there any deceptive statistics or rival causes? Is there any significant information that has been omitted, either carelessly or intentionally, and what other reasonable conclusions are possible?

What Should the Advocates

for Change Ask For?

Clearly, at the K–12 level courses, the goal is to provide the students with a skill set that enables them to exercise critical thinking and to discern fact from propaganda. Another goal is to reintroduce and reinforce courses that provide a clear balance of the rights and responsibilities of citizenship to engage in civil discourse, which is part of civics.

That will benefit our Homelanders and some of the youngest among Millennials. What about the ones who are out of school?

Earlier, we discussed the problem of the young people who are bulk of the active protestors in 2020, and noted that some of them may have participated in criminal behavior, looting, or rioting, even assaulting an officer, or just refusing to abide by legitimate calls by the authorities to go home and behave. What can we do for them?

My recommendation is to use the same approach that the courts use with drivers convicted of driving while intoxicated. Sentence the ones charged with misdemeanor- level behavior to attend a course in civics and critical thinking skills. That means a special program would need to be created that can concisely present the concepts and test the participants on how much of it they have absorbed and comprehend.

I can attest that a course like that would not require more than four or five two-hour sessions that could be presented as adult education in existing public school facilities and provide a certificate of completion to the graduates. An economic incentive might be to relieve the graduates of any pending fines or probation resulting from their previous poor choices. The marginal cost of administering such a program would be a modest compensation package for the instructors. That is certain to be far less than the cost of either incarceration or probation monitoring. And the results are likely to be far longer lasting.

What about those accused and or convicted of more serious offenses? That is beyond the scope of this book, but I suspect that if we are successful in "rehabilitating" minor offenders and getting them to be better citizens who make better life choices, then the professionals responsible for prison administration and probation will take notice and figure out how to implement a similar program for those about to released back into society.

The next step is how to organize and create a powerful group of similarly interested advocates who will generate an enthusiastic positive crusade to improve education and the subsequent social discourse.

CHAPTER 8

Implementing Your Advocacy

Congratulations! You have the tools at your disposal to become an effective education reformer advocate. Now it's up to you to act if you really want there to be a positive change in the educational outcomes of your sons and daughters, their friends, and classmates, and your young adult neighbors to enable them to make better choices based on facts.

It's up to you. I can help. This book has provided the background and general guidance to help you recognize the need for an effective improvement, and a series of facts to build a compelling argument for including critical thinking skills and an increased focus on civics in the education of your children and your neighbors' children. But most of the effort going forward is up to those of you who choose to act decisively and promptly.

The challenge of this book was to use critical thinking in your decision making and to become an advocate. If you chose to simply apply what you have discovered this far in your personal life, then I will consider my efforts to have been productive. As you well know, all decisions have consequences. Applying critical thinking to decision making and carefully evaluating the information upon which we make those daily individual decisions is essential for successful outcomes in business and society at large. If you only apply critical thinking in your everyday decisions, you increase the opportunity for successful results. Your personal and family life will be better for it. But if you want to have a more significant impact, and influence the overall society to make better decisions, then you must take a big step and become an advocate.

Start Now

That means you now must decide to act. Plan the process. Begin the implementation. Do the research to learn the current rules and regulations of your state and district board of education. Document the level of success achieved by the graduates of that system. Identify potential community leaders who share your desire to improve the education system in your area.

Build a consensus.

Personal anecdotal evidence is useful, but insufficient. Engage a group of your neighbors and learn their concerns and issues with the local schools. Share what you've learned from this book and invite them to join you in your efforts to make an effective change in your schools. The power of a group of enthusiastic supporters increases the probability of success exponentially.

Identify the key players

in the decision process and assess which ones are candidates likely to look positively at our request. Note I said "request." Not demand. Decision makers need to be convinced that the current outcomes are incomplete or unsatisfactory and you have a viable solution. Your approach needs to demonstrate how it will benefit them and the students they are responsible for educating.

Depending on the current regulations and course content in your district, the change I've recommended may range from a minor modification and focus to a wholesale change in both content and philosophy. In either case, there are some tools and techniques available that will improve the effectiveness of your process.

Hone Your Leadership Skills

I will summarize some of the key elements and encourage you to apply these proven methods of effective leadership that I have shared with my freshman students. Their feedback indicates the material was not only interesting, but useful, as they proceeded up through their undergraduate program, learned more, and earned better grades with less stress and conflict.

I started with general management concepts in the very first class, introducing Stephen Covey's classic book, *The 7 Habits of Highly Effective People.*[34] The freshman met in small groups to discuss how they could apply those habits to their university studies. Many shared with me how useful that introductory class was for them. At mid-course, my students had studied the various aspects of effective communication and were now responsible to integrate those skills to make effective, short informative presentations. Even the most timid and introverted students managed to put it all together, so I am confident that you will be able to do that too.

Since my Gen X students liked visual learning, I added some YouTube videos by Simon Senik, whose work deals primarily with effective management of Millennials based on his book, *Start with Why.*[35] You can find them easily online if you want some insights on how to encourage and motivate that age group.

Another topic we lightly covered in class was a quick summary of the recommendations for exemplary leadership by two accomplished business professors, Jim Kouzes and Barry Posner. They published a summary of the five key attributes of exemplary leadership: Model the way; Inspire a shared vision; Challenge the process; Enable others to act; Encourage the heart.[36]

Turning the Tables

I have incorporated some of all these management recommendations in my previous chapters, but another key element I propose is a bit more unusual. Central to the argument for improving the educational outcomes is to turn the tables on the resisters and the entrenched bureaucracy and use some of the weapons that successful community organizers have employed for at least fifty years. Those techniques are based on Saul Alinsky's *Rules for Radicals.* Some aspects of his 1971 book are germane today, especially if your neighborhood school includes minority students. The key aspect relevant for our objective is to become an effective community organizer and get your neighbors to become enthusiastic supporters to add critical thinking to the curriculum and to increase the focus in school on the rights and responsibilities of citizenship.

Alinsky's rules have been criticized for creating an "enemy" to be vanquished, but you may discover that there are actually some enemies to be vanquished in changing the curriculum. Not all communities have entrenched resisters to change. But it will take much more than just one lone voice speaking up at a local council meeting. You will need an audience filled with supporters to get the attention of most politicians.

Outreach to Parents

In today's social diversity environment, seek out minority adults with children in your schools. Explain to them how their children will have a better chance of achieving success if they learn the skills of critical thinking and understand the rights and privileges of citizens. Those parents will become some of your most ardent supporters. School boards and education administrators are seeking effective ways to make their programs more "diverse." Provide the decision makers a reason to make critical thinking a way to set their curriculum above the competition.

In his book, the late Stephen Covey recommended to "Always begin with the end in mind." This is one of his *7 Habits* and his material has been at the core of much of the subsequent management literature with contemporary applications by other authors based on improvements in technology and changes in the composition of the workforce. In the previous chapter I provided the outline of how I suggest you prepare to be an effective advocate for the desired addition to the curriculum. When I have used Covey's *7 Habits* in my professional life, the results have always been more predictable and the process easier to manage.

Enthusiasm Works

Every successful marketer knows that enthusiasm sells. Knowledge of your product is crucial to describe the benefits and to overcome objections This is not a product to sell, but a concept that is emotional. Passionately share your goal with your neighbors and your local representatives on the city council and the school board. Challenge them to join the crusade and advocate our mutual goals: The success of our children to be productive, well informed, successful adults. Once you have some commitment from the authorities at the local level, maintain your enthusiastic support. Remain engaged in the process. Be a cheerleader. Be available to help integrate the critical thinking skills into various courses.

KISS

A classic management technique is to "keep it short and simple" (KISS). To overcome resistance, we must make it as easy as possible for the school administration and the teachers tasked with adding the material to their courses. I have created management courses from scratch as training courses for university support staff training (not for the faculty). I have created undergraduate and graduate level courses from little more than a course title and a predetermined objective. If you have those two things—topic and outcome goals —the process is straight forward.

Critical thinking at the K–7 grade levels does not need to be a separate course. It will be easier to get accepted by adding a few lectures with teachers notes and study objectives already prepared for the faculty to incorporate into their existing courses to provide their students with examples of how to apply the concepts. Incorporation could be as simple as one added assignment of some local topic of interest to be discussed in the classroom that demonstrates the way to think critically. We can provide teaching guide with questions and suggested topics. There is no one right answer to most issues. It is a thinking process.

High school sophomores have always been eager to challenge authority. Critical thinking courses at that level should have a deeper analysis and more targeted student assignments to build their skills in applying the concept of asking questions, challenging assumptions, looking for ambiguous words and phrases, and recognizing statistics that may be incomplete or misleading. Make it part of the assignment to delve into the background and experience of the authors of the articles they are analyzing. Especially get them in the habit of investigating the reputation of the person presenting the news to determine if they have the credentials to make the viewer/listener accept what they say as factual. The goal is not to obtain a desired conclusion, but to build the analytical skills of the student. The process is the goal.

In the earlier chapter I suggested an adult education night course for disruptive young people who may have participated in unruly demonstrations. A similar targeted summary of the critical thinking skills would provide a useful assignment for a half day detention study hall assignment.

A course at the university freshman level only needs a two-hour block once or twice a week over the course of a typical semester. The materials I presented in half a dozen classes were just quickly broad-brush overview of the materials. There are easy to read, and utilize relatively inexpensive books that could provide the full course content with topics for discussion and assignments. The teacher does not have to reinvent the wheel to get prepared and build useful skills for their students. Homeschool is ideal for including these concepts.

Instant Homeschooling

In the past year, thousands—perhaps hundreds of thousands—of parents have had to become teachers; home schooling their children who were denied access to classrooms because of the COVID-19 virus and the concerns over infection rates. Schools have always been a petri dish for colds and flu but the facts as noted in previous chapters do not support the isolation of the young students and the refusal of entrenched middle-aged bureaucrats to return to their professional roles physically interacting in a social environment. Adequate protective measures were taken in the early stage of the pandemic in many European countries and US-based private schools. Those measures have demonstrated they were effective and the contagious concerns were overstated. The closing of schools has caused more long-lasting psychological harm to the students and their parents than the virus was likely to do. Some parents have the patience and talent to be effective homeschool teachers. Most do not.

A Teacher's Guide

I refer you back to the first chapter and the discussion of *A Teacher's Guide*. It will help you organize and prepare appropriate lesson plans. It is a Useful and affordable aid.

But for all parents, and teachers, there is a KISS solution I will share with you. Here. Now. Free.

Four Ws of a Respectful Skeptic.

The habits of a critical thinker are based on four simple questions. The goal is to build the habits of politely asking simple questions to become a respectful skeptic.

- Says who?
- Why should I care?
- Why should I believe you?
- Where's the proof?

I have developed a companion text with a brief recap of the issues and a set of lesson plan outlines and a self- evaluation of the class experience in a separate focused text titled *A Teacher's Guide* also available at Amazon.com.

Thank you for making the investment of your time to read my book. I encourage you to put the concepts to work. Start with your own family unit as you watch the evening news. Ask your kids about what they are reading and listening to on their phones and tablets by asking them the basic questions about what they are seeing and being taught. Encourage them by example.

For there to be a significant change there must be a significant effort. A combined cadre of Critical Thinking Advocates is what it will take. If you want to help, please register at BlameItonNam. com and together we can create the momentum to protect our youth's future, have a positive impact on their growth and prosperity, and do the same for their friends and neighbors and the communities in which we all live. Those who are in the United States of America have the privilege of living in one of history's finest social experiments in individual liberty, but it requires an ongoing effort to preserve and defend it.

Please join us. And remember the **Three Ps**: Be Prepared. Be Polite. Be Persistent.

About the Author

I have shared some of my life experiences and alluded to the degrees I've earned and some of the professional experiences I've had in the pages of this book as they relate to the subject. If you read the "Dedication" I disclose that the most satisfying part of teaching is sharing what you know and seeing others succeed.

 One of the most enjoyable 'jobs' I've ever done never earned me a dime. I spent a decade as a volunteer construction supervisor for the Habitat for Humanity chapter in Atlanta when I was a faculty member at Georgia State University. I probably have my blood, sweat and tears in over a hundred homes built for the working poor. My forte was framing and siding. It is an amazing experience to take a group of a dozen volunteers who have little or no construction experience and lead them over two Saturdays to stand up the wall frames other volunteers have created in a warehouse, get them vertical and properly integrated with the roofing trusses, then covered with composite wood siding that

is perfectly horizontal and uniform. To be able to step back with the volunteers and see a house that didn't exist two weekends before is very satisfying. The best part of course, were the big smiles on the faces of the new owners when they were handed the keys and the opportunity to live in something they could call their own.

I have written this book with the same passion to share what I believe parents and teachers have an obligation to give their children: the facts. Provide a framework for responsible decision making and then make informed choices aware of the likely consequences.

If you would like to improve the life skills of our students, your neighbors, and our communities, then I'd very much like to hear from you with your reaction to what I've shared here. Please email me at tom@blameitonnam.com and join the fledgling crusade.

Appendix–An Action Checklist

Plan the process.

Planned start date _____
*Next community meeting date(s) open for discussion*_____
Create a clear goal statement

• Decision makers need to be convinced that the current outcomes are incomplete or unsatisfactory and you have a viable solution.

Identify the key players in the decision process

Assess which ones are candidates likely to look positively at our request.

Your approach needs to demonstrate how it will benefit them and the students they are responsible for educating as noted repeatedly in the previous chapters

Specific Benefits to be derived from implementation

• Save money
• Save time
• Less work for teachers and administrators
• Better communication skills of students

Begin the implementation.

Do the research:

1. Learn the current rules and regulations of your state
2. Regulations of local District board of education.
3. Any local school rules or conflicts with state or district

Document the level of success achieved by the graduates:
Average SAT scores over the past several decades:

	1990	2000	2010	2020
Math	_____
Reading Comprehension	_____

Number of graduates accepted to universities:_____
_____US Top 10 _____State _____U Comm College

Identify potential community leaders who share your desire to improve the education system in your area.
  • Names & ages:

  • Educational background:

  • Work experience: ___Public ___Private Co ___Entrepreneur

Build a consensus.

Personal anecdotal evidence is useful but insufficient. Share what you've learned from this book and invite the neighbors to join you in your efforts to make an effective change that will improve the skills of all your offspring. The power of a group of enthusiastic supporters increases the probability of success exponentially.

Know the details of the following:
_____ Population of your school district
_____ Ethnic composition of the district and the schools
_____ Economic circumstances of the district

Develop your child's story – examples of success and challenges that were or could have been improved with better life skills learned at school.

Engage a group of your neighbors and determine possible 'coffee' conversation dates and times

Identify the politically active individuals in your local community
Name _____Phone_____ email_____

Neighborhood civic groups – where and when they meet and who the leaders are.

Who are the key local teachers or educators?
Names_____ Academic credentials_____
Work history_____

Gather the information on the parents of your child's classmates and the parents of neighbors' children
Names parent & child_____ Phone____ email_____

Schedule informal gatherings in small groups of five or fewer people

- Catalog their concerns and issues with the local schools.
- Identify those eager to be publicly supportive
- Identify those who are supportive but prefer behind the scenes work

Develop your personal action plan.

Establish and commit to a level of advocacy you are comfortable doing.

Prepare your appeal to the key community leaders and get on the agenda for the next available community or school board meeting.

Draft and rehearse a five to ten minute presentation clearly explaining why the life skills should be included in the local curriculum. Be prepared with the facts and data you developed in your research to substantiate and invigorate the discussion.

Close your presentation with a call to action of the leaders of the community and school board. Ask for their public support to improving the educational experience and abilities of the students in their program.

Follow up with the key leaders in two or three days and keep the energy moving in a positive direction to implement the needed improvements and adaptations to the curriculum.

References and Resources

Chapter Two

1 Stephen D. Brookfield, *Developing Critical Thinkers: Challenging Adults to Explore Alternative Ways of Thinking and Acting* (San Francisco, CA: Jossey-Bass Publishers, 1987).

2 Chuck Clayton, *The Re-Discovery of Common Sense! A Guide to: The Lost Art of Critical Thinking* (New York, NY: iUniverse, Inc., 2007).

3 M. Neil Browne and Stuart Keeley, *Asking the Right Questions: A Guide to Critical Thinking,* 8th ed. (Upper Saddle River, NJ: Pearson Prentice Hall, 2006).

4 Lane Wallace, "Multicultural Critical Theory at B-School?" *New York Times,* June 10, 2010, B1, B7.

Chapter Three

5 David Card and Thomas Lemieux, "Going to College to Avoid the Draft: The Unintended Legacy of the Vietnam War," *American Economic Review 91* (2001): 97–102.

6 John C. Fletcher, "Avoidance and the Draft," *Washington Post,* February 25, 1992.

7 Amy Rutenberg, "How the Draft Reshaped America," *New York Times,* October 6, 2017.

8 Robert P. George, "What Causes—and What Might Cure—Illiberalism and Groupthink in Education?" in *How to Educate an American,* ed. Michael J. Petrilli and Chester E. Finn, Jr. (Conshohocken, PA: Templeton Press, 2020), 36–39.

Chapter Four

9 David McCullough, The Pioneers: The Heroic Story of the Settlers Who Brought the American Ideal West (New York, NY: Simon and Schuster, 2019) 29–30.

10 Homeroom, Official Blog of the U.S. Department of Education. Accessed March 18, 2021. https://blog.ed.gov/2015/04/what-is-esea/.

11 Thomas Sowell, Charter Schools and Their Enemies (New York, NY: Hachette Book Group, Inc., 2020), Kindle edition.

12 D. Patrick Saxon and Hunter R. Boylan, "The Cost of Remedial Education in Higher Education," Journal of Developmental Education 25 (Winter 2001): 2–8.

13 Maria Bartiromo, host, "Wall Street Week" with Maria Bartiromo, August 30, 2019. https://www.foxbusiness.com/features/go-to-school-all-day-sal-khan-makes-the-argument-for-it

14 Bill O'Reilly, host, "The O'Reilly Update," podcast, June 17, 2020. https://www.billoreilly.com/b/Radio:-June-17-2020/71479338803654405.html

15 https://en.wikipedia.org/wiki/Whitney_v._California

16 https://1776unites.com/

17 A.L. Kroeber and Talcott Parsons, "The Concepts of Culture and the Social System," American Sociological Review 23 (1958): 582–3.

18 William Strauss and Neil Howe, Generations: The History of America's Future, 1564–2069 (New York, NY: William Morrow and Company, Inc., 1991).

19 William Strauss and Neil Howe, The Fourth Turning: An American Prophecy-What the Cycles of History Tell Us About America's Next Rendezvous with Destiny (New York, NY: Three Rivers Press, 1997).

20 John M. Ellis, The Breakdown of Higher Education: How It Happened, the Damage It Does, and What Can Be Done (New York, NY: Encounter Books, 2020), Kindle edition.

21 Kenneth O'Reilly, Racial Matters: The FBI's Secret File on Black America, 1960-1972 (New York, NY: The Free Press, 1989).

22 Ward Churchill and Jim Vander Wall, The COINTELPRO Papers: Documents from the FBI's Secret Wars Against Dissent in the United States (Boston, MA: South End Press, 1990).

23 Final Report of the Select Committee to Study Governmental Operations with Respect to Intelligence Activities, United States Senate. Archived February 12, 2015, at the Wayback Machine.

Chapter Six

24 "Woodrow Wilson Foundation Finds Only One State Can Pass U.S. Citizenship Exam," The Woodrow Wilson National Fellowship Foundation, press release, February 15, 2019.

25 Adam Meyerson and Adam Kissel, "Philanthropy and the Civic Education Challenge," in How to Educate an American, ed. Michael J. Petrilli and Chester E. Finn, Jr. (Conshohocken, PA: Templeton Press, 2020), 51–64.

26 US Department of Justice, Office of Justice Programs, https://www.ojp.gov/pdf-files/171676.pdf

27 Michael J. Petrilli and Chester E. Finn, Jr., ed., How to Educate an American (Conshohocken, PA: Templeton Press, 2020).

Chapter Seven

28 https://www.statista.com/statistics/241488/population-of-the-us-by-sex-and-age/

29 William Strauss, "Talking about their Generations: Making Sense of a School Environment Made Up of Gen-Xers and Millennials," School Administrator 62 (September 2005): 10.

30 https://issuu.com/sandrarudd/docs/generation_differences

31 Richard Zeoli, 7 Principles of Public Speaking (New York, NY: Skyhorse Publishing, 2006).

Chapter Eight

32 Deborah Roach Gaut and Eileen M. Perrigo, Business and Professional Communication for the 21st Century (Needham Heights, MA: Allyn and Bacon, 1998).

33 Cyndi Maxey and Kevin E. O'Connor, Present like a Pro (New York, NY: St. Martin's Griffin 2006).

34 Stephen R. Covey, The 7 Habits of Highly Effective People (New York, NY: Free Press, 1989).

35 Simon Sinek, Start with Why (New York, NY: Penguin Group Publishing (USA), 2009).

36 James M. Kouzes and Barry Z. Posner, "The Five Practices of Exemplary Leadership" in *The Leadership Challenge: How to Make Extraordinary Things Happen in Organizations*, 6th ed.(Hoboken, NJ: John Wiley & Sons, Inc., 2017).

Made in the USA
Columbia, SC
27 April 2022

59458170R00090